SEALED
WITH A
KISS

D·LIVER · D·BETTER · D·SOONER · LETTER

SWAK

The Complete
Book of Mail
Fun for Kids

Randy Harelson

Workman Publishing, New York

Library of Congress Cataloging in Publication Data
Harelson, Randy.
   SWAK, the complete book of mail fun for kids.
   Summary: Suggests slogans, codes, craft projects,
games, and other activities that can enhance letter
writing.
   1. Letter-writing—Juvenile literature.
[1. Letter writing] I. Title.
PE1483.H28   808.6   80-54624
ISBN 0-89480-150-3 (pbk.)   AACR2

Cover and book design: Randy Harelson
Photospreads: Jerry Darvin

Workman Publishing Company, Inc.
1 West 39 Street
New York, New York 10018

Manufactured in the United States of America
First printing May 1981
10 9 8 7 6 5 4 3 2 1

Many thanks to all my friends and
correspondents who shared their skills,
ideas, and artwork to help create a book
that glows with the generous spirit of
mail art:
The kids who shared their codes, verses,
pictures, and other envelope graffiti—
Heather Binion, Erin Blackwell, Cathy
Christen, Corey Farrands, Tessa Herd,
Marguerite Keiper, Michelle Kraemer,
Anna Kramer, Sonia Krinke, Karyn Long,
Kevin Long, Scott Long, Kristin McCoy,
Randi Meddaugh, Danny Murphy, Brian
Nettles, Debby Reiley, Kathy Schwartz,
Rebecca Stone, Debby Watson, Shelley
Whitman, Brenda Zarek, and Lori Zarek;
And a few adults who still remembered—
E. D. Barnes, Ann Brown, Linda Bruno, and
Patucci Shehan;

The artists who brighten SWAK with their
imaginative, personal, and delightful
images— Rose Avery, Anne Bray, George
(geORge) Brett, Michael Cooper, Jackie
Choinere, Chris Craven, Martin Raul
Eckmeyer, Margo Eglin, Carmen Elliott,
Jack Eaton, James Felter, Harley Francis,
Cyndy Harry, Sean Harwood, E. F. Higgins
III, Brian Jones, Becky Jordan, Studio
LeClair, John Meyers, Gerry Miller, Maria
Natalia, Jean Pinson, Carlo Pittore, Carol
Rizzo, Leah Rosenthal, Marilyn Rosado,

Don Sagramoso, Kim Samas, Michael Scott, Soft-Art Press, Don Tinsley (who had the idea for a mask-postcard), Lisa Turinese, Edgardo-Antonio Vigo, Bill Whorrall, Kim Wilson, Annie Wittels, the late Art Wood, and especially Joan and Elisabeth Ashley, Anna Banana, Vicki Bartolini, Ken Brown, Jocelyn Cohen, Connie Coleman, Richard Craven, Betty Ruth Curtiss, Trudy Bee DeCanio, Rita DeLisi, Clint Harelson, Donald Lipski, Graciela Marx, Marjorie Merena, Nancy Poore, Katherine Sears, Lon and Lee Spiegelman, Carol Stetser, and Chuck Welch, the Cracker Jack Kid;

The rubber stampers — Herb Harrington, Marilyn Housley, Leavenworth Jackson, Jackie Leventhal, J. E. Rossman, Lowry Thompson, and Karen Richards (who had the idea for a SWAK rubber stamp);

The pen pal people who know that communication is the key to world peace — Robert Carroll, John Holland, Margaret MacDonough, Ettie Moscowitz, Neil O'Donnell, Pentti Pirkkala, Julie Smith, and Melinda Greenblatt (who gave me their addresses);

The clubs and collectors — Vaughn H. Augustin, Karen Cartier, Dane S. Claussen, Lynn R. Donahue, B. Ettelson, David Forthoffer, Michael Guy, H. E. Harris, Jr., Marci Helms, Kathryn Johnson, Tom Kielty, Jay Lounsbury, James Lowe, John McNamara, Fred Meyer, Dorothy Nash, C. A. Reiss, Ted Shelton, Jewell Sonderegger, Helen Warren, and William P. York;

The people of the United States Postal Service and Canada Post who make the fun of mail possible — especially William F. Bolger, Harry Kizirian, Ronald Powell, Michael Rapsey, and my mailman, Carl Longo (who delivered most of the stuff in this book);

Finally, all the other special people who helped in many ways — Tom Ahern, Bill Baker, Richard Barone, Charlton Burch, Sue Calderone, Jerry Darvin, Kim Fawl, Annie Fonfa, Bill Gaglione, Pam Golden, Anne Hamilton, Paul Hanson, Jim Harrison, Judith Hoffberg, Anita Jacobson, Tammy Jacobson, Karen Lambe, Nancy Marino, Florence Mayers, Nancy Moorehead, Judy Mulligan, Janice O'Donnell, Wendy Palitz, Kalim Pearson, Marcia Perlmutter, Alan Powell, Bob Rizzo, Richard Rew, J. T. Tatgenhorst, Ludvik Tomazic, Zoe Weaver, and especially Suzanne Rafer (first-class editor) and Richard Gibbs. Sealed with a kiss to every one of you.

To Jack, Wessie, and Clint: my most faithful correspondents.

May, 1981

Dear Mailfriend,

Everybody loves to get mail. Writing <u>SWAK</u> was wonderful because I got to do all the things I wrote about, and the mail I received was terrific (lots of it is pictured in the book). I got airmail letters from pen pals in Ireland and Israel, mail art from Argentina and Indiana, and envelope graffiti from California and New York. I even got a personal letter from William F. Bolger, the postmaster general of the United States. And I made lots of new friends.

<u>SWAK</u> will make your mail more fun, too. It's packed with ideas, activities, and addresses to help you share, play, collect, create, celebrate, and communicate <u>via post</u>!

Share secrets (in code), doodles, jokes, surprises, greetings, and graffiti. Play postal chess and round robins. Join clubs. Send goofy mail to your friends. Collect postage stamps, postmarks, and picture postcards from everywhere. Create sensational stationery with beautiful borders, and decorate envelopes with the full-color cutouts that come with this book. Celebrate birthdays, holidays, and special occasions with great-looking, homemade greeting cards. Find a pen pal. Write to sports heroes, movie stars, the president of the U.S., and your best friends.

Mail makes it possible to explore and interact with every part of the world. But best of all, it's a great way to share friendships.

Have fun!

Yours till Niagara Falls,

Randy

Contents

RULES OF THE GAME

MASTERPIECE MAIL

CELEBRATIONS

COLLECTIONS

PEOPLE TO WRITE

SWAK is filled with ways to get the most out of mail. You can make new friends, meet famous people, build collections, get free stuff, and much more. But first, as in all games, it's best to learn the rules.

To get started you need only a few supplies: envelopes, writing paper, a pen or pencil, first-class stamps, and postal cards (plain white postcards with the stamp printed right on it and sold by the post office for the price of the stamp alone).

FIRST-CLASS MAIL

For the activities you'll find in *SWAK* always use first-class mail. First-class is for personal correspondence (mostly hand-written or typed cards and letters), and it gets the fastest, most careful service by the people at the post office. It's also private and may not be opened for inspection.

Second-, third-, and fourth-class mail are used mainly in business.

The Mail Must Get Through . . . the Postal Machines

In modern post offices much of the work of sorting, canceling, and even reading typed addresses on mail, is done by machines. Store-bought envelopes, stationery, postcards, and greeting cards all come in standard sizes and go easily through the postal machines. On the other hand, an 8-by-10-inch glossy photo of your favorite movie star, for instance, won't fit—and you certainly don't want to fold it! Never fear, it's mailable. Flat mail taller than 6⅛ inches or longer than 11½ inches is called "nonstandard" and requires some extra postage since it must be handled separately. Take nonstandard mail to a post office where a postal clerk can tell you exactly how much postage to buy.

Make a Nonstandard Mail Guide

Cut a piece of cardboard into a rectangle 6⅛ inches by 11½ inches. By comparing pieces of mail to this guide you can tell whether they require extra postage. Keep it handy with your stationery and mail supplies.

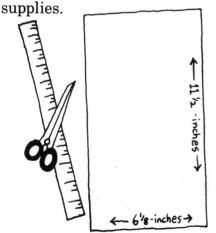

← 11½ inches →

← 6⅛ inches →

Mailing an Elephant

The cost of mailing something depends mainly on how much it weighs; the heavier it is, the more postage it requires.

Your family may own a small postal scale, available at dime stores for about $3.50. If so, ask someone to explain its use. With a scale you can be certain to use the right amount of postage.

The cost is figured by the ounce or by grams. An average card or letter weighs less than an ounce (an ounce is 30 grams) and therefore needs only one first-class stamp.

Of course, if you want to mail an elephant *don't* put him on your postal scale (crunch!). You'll also have trouble fitting him through the mail slot at the post office. In other words, take heavy mail items to the post office for weighing.

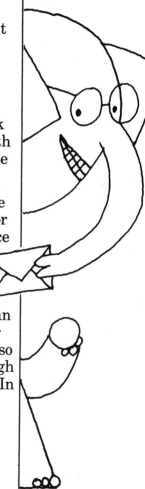

Mini-Mail

When you start making your own postcards (see page 56), the minimum size guide below will come in handy. The United States Postal Service (USPS) accepts no mail smaller than 3½ inches tall by 5 inches long. Smaller pieces might get stuck in postal machines or just get lost.

But of course you can still send tiny letters, bubble gum cards, or a shower of confetti through the mail; all you have to do is put your mini-mail in a standard envelope.

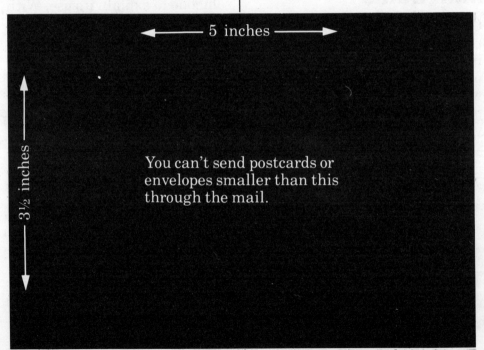

← 5 inches →

3½ inches

You can't send postcards or envelopes smaller than this through the mail.

Proper Address

Besides the correct postage, every envelope should include the destination address and your return address.

Both the destination address and the return address should include:

1. Full name.
2. Street address, post office box, or rural route number (in the case of office buildings, apartment houses, or other multi-unit dwellings the number of the specific apartment or office should be placed to the right of the street address).
3. City, state, ZIP code (in Canada: city, province, and, on a fourth line, the Postal Code).

Use this envelope as a guide to the correct placement of:

YOUR
RETURN
ADDRESS

DESTINATION
ADDRESS

POSTAGE

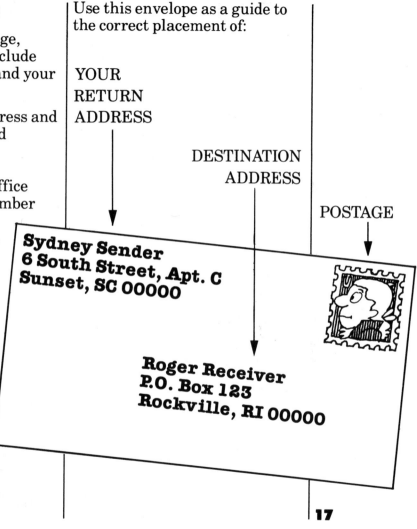

Sydney Sender
6 South Street, Apt. C
Sunset, SC 00000

Roger Receiver
P.O. Box 123
Rockville, RI 00000

Address Abbreviations

These lists show abbreviations preferred by USPS and Canada Post.

Avenue	Ave.	Parkway	Pky.
Boulevard	Blvd.	Plaza	Plz.
Drive	Dr.	Ridge	Rdg.
East	E.	River	Rv.
Expressway	Expy.	Rural	R.
Heights	Hts.	Shore	Sh.
Hospital	Hosp.	South	S.
Institute	Inst.	Square	Sq.
Junction	Jct.	Station	Sta.
Lake	Lk.	Street	St.
Lakes	Lks.	Terrace	Ter.
Lane	La.	Turnpike	Tpke.
Meadows	Mdws.	Union	Un.
North	N.	View	Vw.
Palms	Plms.	Village	Vlg.
Park	Pk.	West	W.

USPS American State and Possession Abbreviations:

Alabama	AL	Missouri	MO
Alaska	AK	Montana	MT
Arizona	AZ	Nebraska	NE
Arkansas	AR	Nevada	NV
California	CA	New Hampshire	NH
Colorado	CO	New Jersey	NJ
Connecticut	CT	New Mexico	NM
Delaware	DE	New York	NY
District		North Carolina	NC
of Columbia	DC	North Dakota	ND
Florida	FL	Ohio	OH
Georgia	GA	Oklahoma	OK
Guam	GU	Oregon	OR
Hawaii	HI	Pennsylvania	PA
Idaho	ID	Puerto Rico	PR
Illinois	IL	Rhode Island	RI
Indiana	IN	South Carolina	SC
Iowa	IA	South Dakota	SD
Kansas	KS	Tennessee	TN
Kentucky	KY	Texas	TX
Louisiana	LA	Utah	UT
Maine	ME	Vermont	VT
Maryland	MD	Virginia	VA
Massachusetts	MA	Virgin Islands	VI
Michigan	MI	Washington	WA
Minnesota	MN	West Virginia	WV
Mississippi	MS	Wisconsin	WI
		Wyoming	WY

Canadian Province and Territory Abbreviations:

Alberta	AB	Nova Scotia	NS
British		Ontario	ON
Columbia	BC	Prince Edward	
Labrador	LB	Island	PE
Manitoba	MB	Quebec	QC
Newfoundland	NF	Saskatchewan	SK
New Brunswick	NB	Yukon Territory	YT
Northwest			
Territories	NT		

Q. Why did the moron chew up the stamp?
A. It had gum on the back.

ZIP

ZIP Code is a number-language that postal machines "read."

Your ZIP identifies where you receive your mail. The five digits represent the post office in your town or area that handles your mail. The ZIP Code follows the city and state in the last line of every U.S. address.

Before too long, the post office may be revising the ZIP code system to include four *more* numbers. These last four will represent a small area that includes your home or mailbox.

Canada uses a similar number/letter-language called the Postal Code. The first three characters identify a large area, the last three narrow the destination almost to a specific address.

The Postal Code stands alone as the last line of every Canadian address.

What Happens to Your Letter Once You've Dropped It in a Mailbox?

1. First, it's collected by a postal worker and taken to a large nearby post office. There it is sorted according to size, weight, and class.
2. A canceling machine cancels the stamp.
3. Another machine reads the typed code. (Mail without a code is sorted by hand.)
4. A letter-sorting machine puts your letter with other mail headed for the same general destination.
5. Those letters go together into a bag or container that is sent by airplane, truck, or train to the post office nearest that destination.
6. At the destination post office your letter is once again sorted with others headed for the same neighborhood, and finally delivered by a letter carrier.

19

GOOD FORM

People have been writing letters for so long that certain customs have developed; like this basic form for a friendly letter:

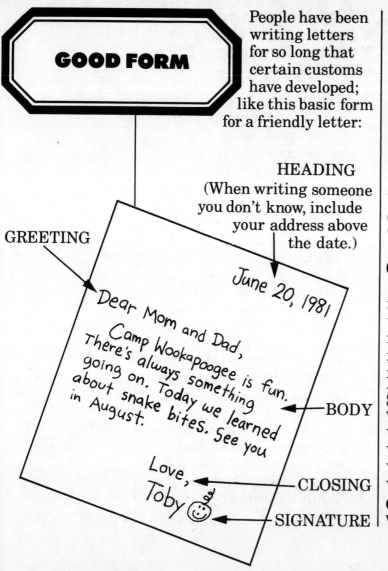

GREETING

HEADING
(When writing someone you don't know, include your address above the date.)

June 20, 1981

Dear Mom and Dad,
Camp Wookapoogee is fun. There's always something going on. Today we learned about snake bites. See you in August.

Love,
Toby

BODY

CLOSING

SIGNATURE

Greetings

Dear _____,
Dearest _____,
Dear People: (business)
Dear Sir,
Dear Madam,
_____, (Deer)
Hello,
Hi!
What's hap'nin'?
Que pasa?
To Whom It May Concern:

Closings

Always,
Best wishes,
As ever,
Love,
Love and kisses,
XOXOXO, (hugs and kisses)
Sincerely,
With all good wishes,
Yours truly,
Very truly yours,
Your friend,
Your pal,
C-ya,
WBS, (Write Back Soon)

Messages to the Postperson

Messages on the backs of envelopes, written to the letter carrier or to the postal service in general may or may not ever get read by postal employees, but they're fun!

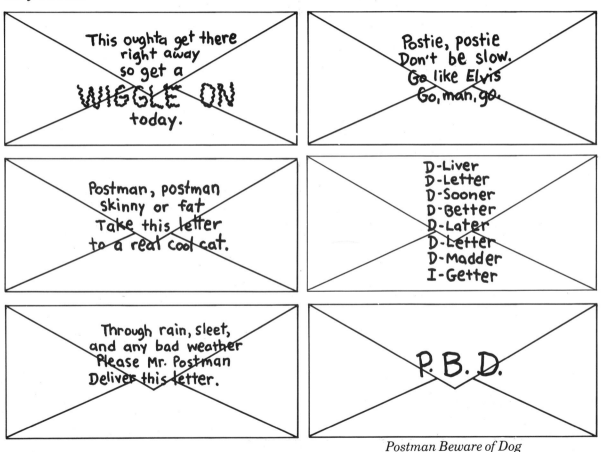

This oughta get there
right away
so get a
WIGGLE ON
today.

Postie, postie
Don't be slow.
Go like Elvis
Go, man, go.

Postman, postman
skinny or fat
Take this letter
to a real cool cat.

D-Liver
D-Letter
D-Sooner
D-Better
D-Later
D-Letter
D-Madder
I-Getter

Through rain, sleet,
and any bad weather
Please Mr. Postman
Deliver this letter.

P.B.D.

Postman Beware of Dog

KEY TO THE ACTIVITIES IN SWAK

You may send either a postcard or a letter.

Throughout this book each little drawing of an envelope like the ones here is a signal of some sort of mail exchange: you send something, then you get something back. When an offer interests you, follow the directions carefully. The drawing is a reminder of what you should send.

Send a letter along with whatever else is requested.

Money is required for purchasing, postage, or handling. Tape coin or coins to your letter (never send money attached to a postcard). If there is more than one coin to send, tape them side by side, not one on top of the other.

What's a SASE (pronounced SAY-zee)?

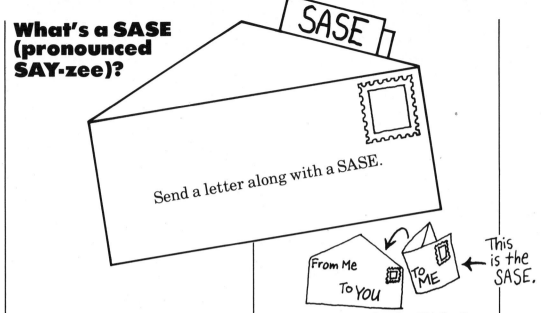

Send a letter along with a SASE.

This is the SASE.

From Me To YOU

TO ME

A SASE is a *Self-A*ddressed *S*tamped *E*nvelope. That means:

1. You address a standard 9-inch envelope *to yourself.*
2. You put a first-class stamp on it.
3. You fold it and put it inside another envelope along with your request. The person you send it to will use your SASE to send something back to you. *Always* use a SASE if it's requested.

If you live outside the United States and want to send a SASE to the U.S., address the envelope to yourself but *do not* add the stamp. Instead, buy an international reply coupon at the post office and include it with your letter and self-addressed envelope. (The person who receives the international reply coupon will exchange it for U.S. stamps at his or her local post office.)

23

Masterpiece
Mail

Most of the supplies needed to create great things to send through the mail are already in your home: envelopes, postage stamps, pens, pencils, scissors, white glue, a ruler, and paper. Some things—things that might otherwise be thrown away—should also be put with your art supplies: greeting cards other people send, used gift wrap and ribbons, cardboard, and out-of-date magazines and catalogs to cut up. (Monster and movie magazines, especially, have great pictures for mail art. Seed catalogs too; look in any gardening magazine for addresses to write to for free flower and vegetable seed catalogs.)

Additional Materials

What follows is a list of additional tools and materials you may wish to keep on hand. They are available at most stationery and dime stores.

26

■ Set of soft-tip pens in rainbow colors.
(Always remember to put the caps on pens immediately after use to keep them from drying out.)

■ Double-stick tape.
(A very neat adhesive for small "stick-together" jobs.)

■ Peel-and-stick address labels.

■ Assorted decorative seals and stickers.

♥ ABC ♥

■ Rubber stamps and ink pads.
(Rubber stamp alphabets are sold in many dime stores for about $2. Picture stamps can be found in some toy and gift shops or ordered from companies like Inkadinkado (page 79), Herb Harrington (page 116), Hero Arts (page 117), or The Rubber Stamp Catalog, P.O. Box 209, Bristol, RI 02809 (catalog $1).

Any piece of paper can become stationery. If it's plain, decorate it. Add borders, a logo, a letterhead, or pictures. If it's already decorated, decorate it some more (add your own "personal touch")! Cut it into different shapes for different occasions, and write your letters in various colored inks to suit your mood.

Pick Your Paper

All sizes of memo pads and writing tablets, lined or unlined, are inexpensive and make good stationery. Graph paper is great. Typewriter paper may be just your "type." And these plain papers are ready and waiting for you to create with felt-tip pens, colored pencils, crayons, rubber stamps, and/or stickers.

Giant Letters

Why not write a letter three feet tall? Use a piece of easel paper or newsprint, both available at art supply stores. Write as large or as small as you like. Mail your massive message in an oversized manila envelope.

Mini-Messages

Little memo pads cost about a quarter each at any dime store and make marvelous mini-stationery. Write the letter in your tiniest handwriting, using a fine-point pen or very sharp pencil. The letter won't even need folding to fit in a standard envelope.

Q. What did the lovesick stamp say to the envelope?
A. "I'm stuck on you."

Create Your Own Logo

A logo is a personal emblem or symbol that identifies its owner. Most organizations—corporations, countries, sport teams and clubs—have logos. (Canada's logo is the maple leaf; NBC-TV's is a peacock and a bold letter N.) You can make up a personal logo using the initial letters of your name or a picture-symbol of your favorite hobby or special interest.

Doodle lots of ideas on scratch paper; once you hit upon something you really like, redo it making it simpler, clearer, and easier to draw. Put your logo on stationery and the flaps of matching envelopes.

Official Letterhead Stationery

A letterhead is a name and address or other heading printed on stationery. It may include your logo. For official-looking writing paper for your family, your club, or yourself, make up a letterhead.

Start by making up a name for your room or house (Jim's Junkheap, The Smith Spread, The Lambe Lodge, Robin's Roost). One of the following words may work well in combination with your name: abode, bunk, castle, cave, chambers, den, dwelling, habitat, hacienda, hangout, home sweet home, homestead, joint, lair, lodge, nest, nook, palace, perch, place, quarters, residence, room, roost, spread.

Once you have made up what your letterhead will say, design your stationery. A letterhead is usually at the top of the paper, centered, or to one side.

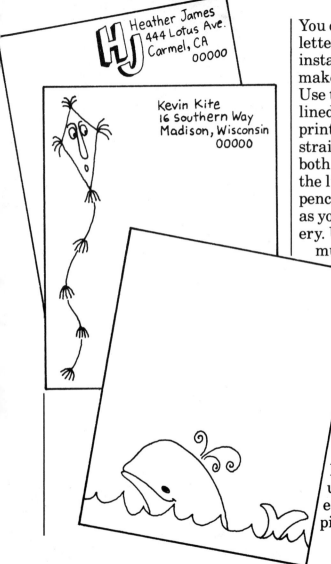

You can make copies of your letterhead stationery on an instant copier, but first you must make one perfect sheet to copy. Use tracing paper. Put a sheet of lined paper underneath so your printing will be even and straight. Tape the corners of both papers to your desk to keep the lines from moving. Lightly pencil in your letterhead exactly as you want it on your stationery. Use a clean eraser if you must erase — smudges of any kind will show up on copies. Go over the penciled letters with a black fine-point felt-tip pen. Carefully remove the tape, and you're ready to print.

Instant Copiers: Mail Art Printshop

Instant copiers are very useful to mail artists — an easy way to make many pieces of stationery (or anything) from a single design. With about three million instant copy machines in the United States, almost everyone can become his or her own printing company. Copy machines (often called Xerox machines — the brand name of the original instant copier) are found in most offices, libraries, and post offices. The cost is from 5¢ to 20¢ per black-and-white copy, for either typewriter-paper size (8½ by 11 inches) or legal size (8½ by 14 inches).

Just place your design face down on the machine's glass plate, close the cover, put in your money, and push the button. (Directions are printed on each machine.) You have your copy in less than a minute.

Also, many small businesses specialize in instant printing and their prices are often cheaper than self-operated machines.

30 You can add color to instant

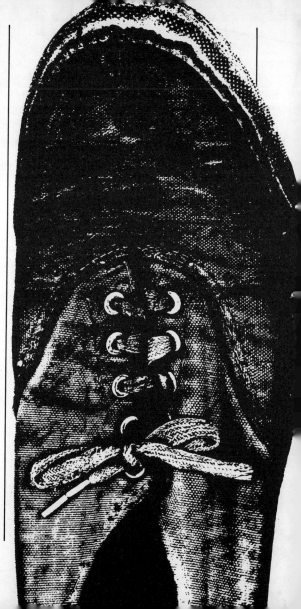

copies with felt-tip pens, colored pencils, or crayons. (There is a color instant copier too, but copies usually cost more than a dollar apiece.)

Instant Artist

Betty Ruth Curtiss is a New Jersey artist who makes her art on instant copiers. She puts slices of bread on the machine and turns the copies into notepaper. She unfolds striped cloth onto the copier's glass plate and uses the copies as lined stationery. After copying a real tennis shoe, she glues the copy onto heavier paper and cuts it out to make an oddly shaped, funny postcard.

As you can see, the art is in the imagination of the artist in choosing *what* to copy and how to use the copy once it is made.

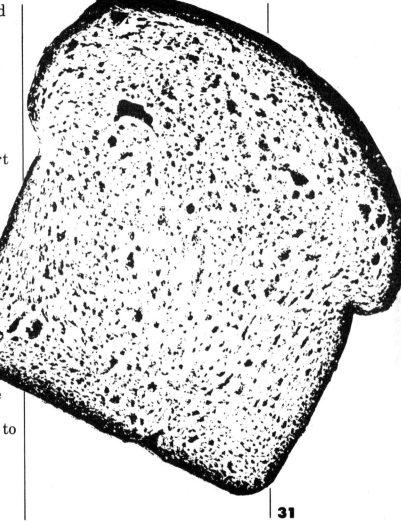

Waxed Stationery ... and Other Kitchen Finds!

Your kitchen is full of the makings of oddball notepapers. Waxed paper and aluminum foil make strange but terrific stationery. Both papers can be cut to any size with scissors, and require permanent-ink felt-tip pens for clear writing. (Water-based ink just won't stick.) A letter on foil written in blue ink looks like outer-space mail.

Brown paper grocery bags recycle into excellent notepaper. Trace around a piece of store-bought stationery several times on one grocery bag. Leave the zigzag edge of the bag as the top edge of the notepaper. Write your note in black ink. If you write on only one side, this stationery doesn't need an envelope. Just fold it twice and seal the flap with tape or a sticker. Address and stamp the other side.

Oztationery

Fred Meyer, secretary of the International Wizard of Oz Club, made up his own Oz stationery to use when writing to club members, Oz fanciers, and—who knows—maybe even the wizard himself! If the Oz books are favorites of yours, Fred will share his stash of stationery with you, and send you information about his club. Write to:

Fred M. Meyer
Int'l Wizard of Oz Club
220 N. Eleventh St.
Escanaba, MI 49829

Ask for a few sheets of Oz stationery, print your name and address neatly, and enclose two first-class stamps.

Easy-to-make decorative borders turn plain paper into sensational stationery. A border can be drawn, colored, stamped, or printed.

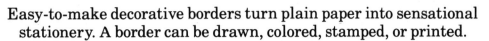

Alternate two simple symbols in different colors to make a pattern.

Alternate stars and bats. Add a dark background.
(An edge of night? Ugh! "Borderline" humor.)

Color-in alternating squares around the edge of graph paper to make a checkerboarder. Fancier geometric borders can also be created.

Small rubber stamps and a stamp pad make for speedy borders. Make a parade of cartoon animals along one edge, or draw a string of colored beads to surround the message. A chorus line of birds would add a cheery note. How about a border of flowers or radishes?

The possibilities are endless.

Rainbow Mail

Even letters written on plain white paper can be colorful and surprising to the eye. Imagine a Christmas letter written in alternating colors. First line red, second line green, then red, then green, and so on till the end. It's a simple idea, but the letter becomes a beautiful pattern of colored stripes.

Felt-tip and other soft-tip pens come in every color of the rainbow and a few colors that aren't even *there*! Even inexpensive ball-point pens come in red, purple, blue, green, and black. Color your letters happy by writing in the color of a special holiday (pink or red in February, green in March) or by alternating seasonal colors (red and blue in June and July, black and orange in October).

Perhaps the most special "colored-ink letter" uses the colors of a real rainbow in spectrum order.

Good Shape

Trim pieces of plain paper into large, simple shapes on which to write to special people: A movie actor on a paper star, a loved one on a big heart, a sailor on ship-shape stationery. Use your scissors and your imagination.

Trace around a bowl or plate to make round stationery. Write on it by turning the circle and spiraling your message toward the center. (On the envelope write: "I finally got *around* to writing.")

34

When you want to make a letter really private, substitute other symbols for letters of the alphabet — in other words, write in code. Use the one below or make up your own.

Code					
		M ⊞		**T** +	
A △	**G** ⊖	**N** ⊠	**U** ⌵		
B :	**H** ⊓	**O** •	**V** ∧		
C ⊙	**I** —	**P** ∏	**W** ⋈		
D ▽	**J** ⊔	**Q** ⊗	**X** ⊕		
E ⊟	**K** ⋉	**R** ♀	**Y** ⌂		
F ▢	**L** ⊥	**S** ⊡	**Z** ⊘		

Remember, the person who receives your letter must have a copy of the code to be able to decipher your message.

When You're Up for a Caper Use Paste and Paper

In movie mysteries, people often receive messages spelled out in letters and words clipped from newspapers or magazine headlines and rearranged to say things like "You're next!" or "The butler did it." The idea is that nobody can recognize the handwriting (because there isn't any) and even the FBI can't trace a typewriter that wasn't used. So, when you want to remain anonymous (especially for "guess who" valentines and love letters) use . . .

But make only short messages this way — cutting out and gluing down all those letters takes a long time!

Secrets Inside, Secrets Outside

Don't keep these mysteries to yourself. Use them on envelopes to your under-cover correspondents.

Caution, I Have A Dirty Mind

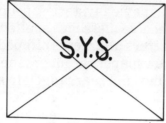

See You Soon

Keep This Under Your Hat

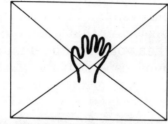

HAND: Have A Nice Day

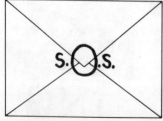

Seal of Secrecy (press the O in sealing wax)

Meet at Clubhouse

Write in Reverse

Write your message backward, then let the receiver figure out how to read it. Position your stationery so you can see it clearly in a mirror. A rectangular mirror held next to your paper is simplest.

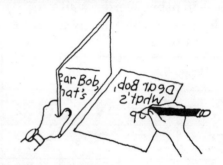

Write so that your message checks out correctly in the mirror. This is tricky but fun. After a while you'll be able to write backward without the mirror.

S.I.E. / S.U.S.

1. S.I.E. (Secrets Inside Envelope) Open up an envelope wide, and print very small

along the bottom crease inside the envelope. Only someone who knows to look there will ever see it.

2. S.U.S. (Secrets Under Stamp) Write your secret very small on the back of a postage stamp. Use a ball-point pen or other waterproof ink. (Test your pen by marking scrap paper, then running water over the mark. If it gets blurry the ink is *not* waterproof.) To stick the stamp on the envelope, moisten it with a wet finger or damp sponge instead of your tongue. The person who gets the letter will have to soak the envelope in cool water before peeling off the stamp and reading the confidential information.

Before sending secrets in these ways, make sure your correspondent knows the meaning of the codes (S.I.E. and S.U.S.) then write the appropriate code on the flap of the envelope.

Say What You Think in Invisible Ink

This is the most secret method of all. The receiver will need to know ahead of time that an invisible message is coming and how to make it become visible.

Use a very clean drawing pen or a toothpick to write your message. Lemon juice, grapefruit juice, or milk work as invisible ink. Dip the "pen" in the "ink" after every three or four letters you write. Use matte (not shiny) paper so the ink soaks in and disappears.

To avoid suspicion, write a regular letter in pen or pencil, then write your invisible message between the lines.

To make it visible, press the paper with a warm iron, or move it around close to an electric light bulb. Heat makes the message appear like magic.

37

PUZZLETTERS

Here's a kind of letter that's easy to write but much harder to read.

It's a kind of maze through which your correspondent must find his or her way in order to get the message. Use a piece of graph paper with at least ¼-inch squares. Write your message by printing one character in a square, moving right, left, up or down to an adjoining square for the next letter. (Do not move diagonally.) Do not leave empty squares between words, but do include punctuation. Read your way through this example maze: Leave blank squares empty or color them in to make the maze a little easier to go through.

D	e	a	r	B	u	d	d	y	,
		y	e	c					T
d	n		o		n	O			h
y	i	f	u			.	e	z	i
o			y	t				a	s
u	r	w	a	o		s	a	m	l
k	c		h	t		i			e
t	a		e			r	e	t	t
o	b		e	n	d	,			
m	r	e	t	t		w	r	i	t
e			e	l	e			a	e
.	u	r	i	e	n	z	a	m	
Y	o	f	r		d	,	T	o	m

D	e	a	r	B	u	d	d	y	,
■	■	y	e	c	■	■	■	■	T
d	n	■	o	■	n	O	■	■	h
y	i	f	u	■	■	.	e	z	i
o	■	■	y	t	■	■	■	a	s
u	r	w	a	o	■	s	a	m	l
k	c	■	h	t	■	i	■	■	e
t	a	■	e	■	■	r	e	t	t
o	b	■	e	n	d	,	■	■	■
m	r	e	t	t	■	w	r	i	t
e	■	■	e	l	e	■	■	a	e
.	u	r	i	e	n	z	a	m	■
Y	o	f	r	■	d	,	T	o	m

Jigsaw Puzzletters

Write a letter on stiff paper, lightweight poster board, or an index card. Then cut it into no more than 12 sharply curved pieces. Put all the pieces into one envelope to mail the letter.

Carol Stetser of Oatman, Arizona, made this birthday puzzle card. She wrote "Happy Birthday, Jim" over and over across the piece of poster board, then drew a large 9 (Jim's age) in pink covering the card's center. Carol cut it into puzzle pieces with scissors before mailing.

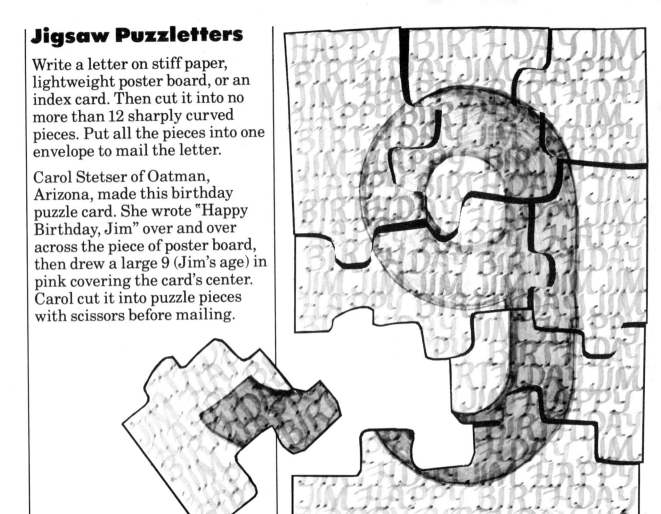

Rebuses on the Outside

Rebuses have always been popular, and have shown up on the envelopes of kids' letters for years.

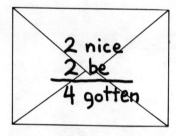

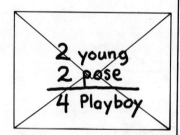

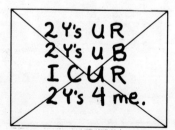

Rebus Letters

A rebus letter is as much fun to write as it is to read. This very old puzzle form uses pictures in place of syllables or words (a picture of a deer means "dear"; an arrow pointing right means "write" or "right"), big letters in place of syllables or words (U means "you"; UU means "use"), and placement of the parts often changes the meaning (a drawing of a comb over a 2 means "come over to . . .").

Spacing is very important in a rebus. Draw and write parts of the same word close together, but leave plenty of space between words.

A rubber stamp alphabet was used to print the big letters in this rebus. Try to read it before checking out the solution.

As you make up rebuses, keep a list of the words and phrases you invent pictures for.

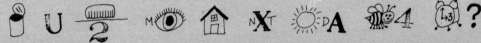

Solution

Dear Pen Pal,

Hello! This letter is a rebus. I think it is fun to write letters this way. What do you think? Why not write one back to me?

Can you come over to my house next Sunday before three o'clock? If you can understand this letter you are mighty smart. Wise guy!

Catch you later,
Randy

Chess by Mail

Did you know that many serious chess players play through the mail? Postal chess is played by two people sending moves written in standard chess notation back and forth to each other through a postal chess club.

If you're an interested chess player, write for more information to one of the following clubs:

Helen Warren, tournament director of APCT says, "Young people love chess by mail — it sharpens their over-the-board game, gives them the chance to meet new friends in other parts of the country, and provides a challenge." When writing to APCT ask for a sample bulletin, book list, and brochure.

**David Forthoffer
Zugzwang! Postal Chess
P.O. Box 21650
San Jose, CA 95151**

**Helen E. Warren
American Postal Chess
Tournaments
P.O. Box 70
Western Springs, IL 60558**

When writing to Zugzwang! please state your age. Ask for the Zugzwang! club bulletin and a flyer explaining their rules for postal chess.

Dungeons, Dragons and Cosmic Encounters

Anyone interested in role-playing games of every description (like Dungeons & Dragons) should know about the *Phantasy Network Newsletter* —completely written, illustrated, and published by folks under the age of 21. The Phantasy Network's purpose is communication among Game Masters and players all over the country.

For more information about the newsletter or about role-playing games in general, send your request and a SASE to:

Happy Hobbit Day!

If you have read and loved J.R.R. Tolkien's books *The Hobbit* and *The Lord of the Rings*, you may be interested in this club.

September 22 is Hobbit Day, and members of the American Tolkien Society send greeting cards to one another to celebrate the occasion. According to ATS secretary Marci Helms, they also have the "hobbit" of scrawling "Frodo Lives," "Sauron Sleeps with a Nightlight," "Visit Scenic Mordor," and "Gandalf for President" on the outside of letters.

Write for more information to:

SASE

American Tolkien Society
P.O. Box 277
Union Lake, MI 48085

Phantasy Network Newsletter
3076 Mercedes Ave.
Davis, CA 95616

CLEARED RATU MAIL SERVICE
358298-1 ****************

IMPERIAL MAIL

PIRATE POSTAL

US MAIL

Blow-dry wookie

Correllian Postage

"Pony Express"
Tatooine style

Fantasy Exchanges

Books and movies, especially ones that create exciting fantasy worlds of their own, sometimes inspire mail exchanges among their more imaginative fans. Lovers of science fiction have been sending "intergalactic mail" for years. *Star Wars* fueled the imaginations of the artists who created the envelopes pictured here. In addition to actual postage, they carry stamps and postmarks from other solar systems.

APPROVED IMPERIAL POSTAL

Add to the fun by choosing or making up a fake name ("mail handle") to use in your fantasy exchange. Call yourself by the name of a favorite fictional character or add a title or some descriptive words to your own and your friend's name (Star Troupe Commander K.D. Jones or Kelly "K-2603" Smith).

Monkeyshine Mail

Q. How can you actually touch someone miles and miles away?

A. You can pull his leg.

No joke: Here are a few zany pranks you can play through the mail.

- Cut a piece of fishing line or string about a yard long. Put it in an envelope with a note that says, "Just thought I'd drop you a line . . ."
- Seal an empty envelope and address it to your friend. On the back write:

Contents:
Magic Disappearing Letter—
Open within the next 2 seconds or the letter will disappear.

- Fold a letter into a paper airplane before putting it into an envelope. Write on the back of the envelope: "Air Mail Inside."

Dear Fri...

U.S. AIRMAIL

- Blow up a balloon about half-full. Write a message on it with felt-tip pen, then let the air out. Put it in an envelope marked "Air Mail Inside." (Balloons like this also make good party invitations.)
- To rib a friend who hasn't written lately, address and stamp an envelope to yourself (a SASE). Put it in an envelope addressed to your friend along with a small note that says, "Your turn."

DECORATE STORE-BOUGHT ENVELOPES

Plain white paper envelopes don't have to stay plain; they can be made as beautiful, funny, mysterious, playful, and creative as their contents—or more so. As long as you keep the destination address clearly readable you may decorate envelopes in whatever wonderful ways your imagination can dream up.

Robin G.
"The Meadows"
14 Feather La.
Lark, CA
00000

Molly Dare
20 Raintree Ter.
Monroe, SC 00000

An envelope must carry the postage and address for postal employees to see and read easily, but it may also carry stickers, cartoons, collage, codes, and other decoration.

The flap side of an envelope may be covered with pictures, patterns, words, and anything else.

Extend a Stamp

Commemorative postage stamps are colorful and decorative in themselves. An easy way to dress up an envelope is simply to pick out the main color(s) in the stamp you're using and write the address in ink of the same color(s).

You might also use the picture on the postage stamp as the idea for your envelope decoration. For example, if the stamp pictures a fish you could draw fish swimming all around the address.

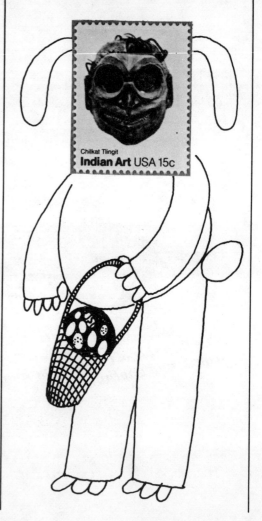

When the picture on a stamp looks like part of a larger scene, draw the rest of the scene (from your imagination) right on the envelope. (*Do not* draw on the stamp itself or postal workers may think it has already been used and postmarked.) Color the scene with pens or pencils in the colors that are on the stamp.

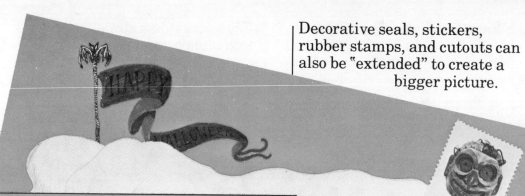

Decorative seals, stickers, rubber stamps, and cutouts can also be "extended" to create a bigger picture.

Sealed with a Cat

Many organizations (the National Wildlife Federation, the American Lung Association, Greenpeace, and the Cousteau Society, for example) publish decorative stamps (such as Christmas Seals) for their members and other people to use on cards and letters. The seals help publicize each organization's name and goals.

Some of the loveliest stamps are put out by Pet Pride, a national humane foundation dedicated to the care, protection, and improved status of cats. Their stamps picture cats of various breeds in full color. If you're a cat lover write for a free sheet of forty stamps to:

Pet Pride
15113 Sunset Blvd.
Pacific Palisades, CA 90272

The Envelope and Its Muddy Ancestor

Although paper envelopes are fairly new in the history of mail, the ancient Babylonians used a sort of envelope thousands of years ago. After a letter had been carved into a stone or clay tablet, the tablet was covered with mud to protect the writing and keep the message private. (Imagine getting one of *those* in your mailbox!) Paper envelopes didn't come into general use until after the invention of adhesive postage stamps and the introduction of the penny post in Great Britain in 1840. Before that post offices charged extra for "any paper enclosed in another" so people just wrote the name and address on back of the folded letter.

On the Flap Side

Lots of jokes, pictures, and messages kids write on the backs of envelopes have been around a long time. Your parents may have written them on letters when they were kids. Ask if they remember any from . . . way . . . back . . . then.

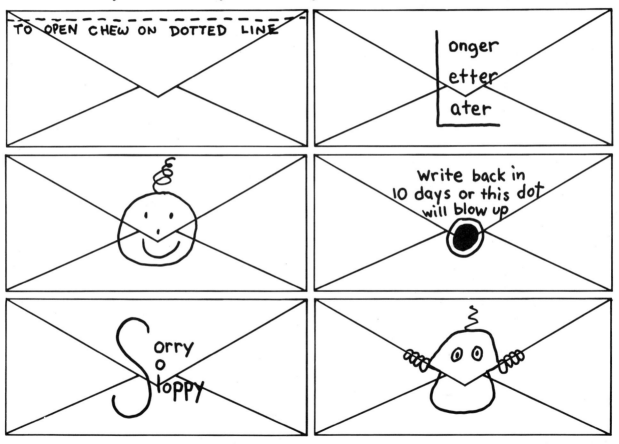

Dress up a homemade card or special letter by sending it in a colorful, patterned paper envelope. Make it from recycled gift wrap, a colorful bag, or any paper you like.

1. Find a store-bought envelope that fits your card or stationery.
2. Slowly and carefully (a) pull the glued tabs of the envelope apart so you can (b) open the entire piece flat. Now you have your tracing shape. This can be used again and again, so keep it with your supplies.

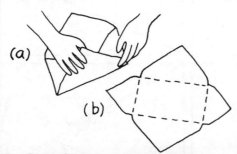

3. Lay the opened envelope on the back of your piece of patterned paper. (One edge of the envelope should line up with one edge of the patterned paper. This way there's less waste, and you may be able to make several envelopes from one piece of paper.)
4. Use two small pieces of tape to keep the envelope in place on the paper.

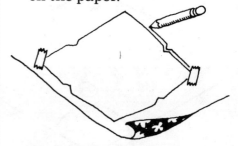

5. Trace around the envelope with a pencil.
6. Remove the tape. Cut out the envelope shape from the patterned paper.
7. Fold the new, fancy envelope together using the original as a guide.

54

8. Use very small dots of white glue to hold the tabs together.

9. Seal the flap closed with a sticker or a bit of glue.

GLUE!

Fold up

An envelope doesn't have to be the store-bought paper kind; it can also be made from a recycled paper or plastic bag, scrap cloth stitched to make a pocket, a Sunday color comic or magazine page folded and taped, or any covering that will hold the contents and protect them through the bumpy postal journey.

HAPPY BIRTHDAY

15¢ OLIVER WENDELL HOLMES

For Name And Address Use a Gummed Label.

MAKE POSTCARDS

OINK · PIG · POSTCARD · OINK · PIG · POSTCARD ·

POST CARD

Dear U,
   The message you are reading is on the back of a homemade picture postcard cut from a single sturdy piece of cardboard or poster board. The picture is drawn, taped, or glued onto the other side.
   This side gets the message, name and address, and the stamp.
   Postcards are easy and fun to make, and you don't have to say much. Lots of ideas for making your own are pictured on the next few pages.

SWAK

U. D. Reader
Yorr House
Hometown, OK
   00000

Your Own™ Professional Postcards

Rita DeLisi has come up with a no glue/no mess method for making your own one-of-a-kind postcards. Her company, Littlehouse, produces and sells self-stick blank postcard "backs" —all you do is peel off the protective cover and stick on whatever "front" you like. With these sticky backs you can recycle magazine pictures, scrap fabric, your artwork, already-used cards, or anything you can think of. Trim the front with scissors to complete your very professional-looking card. For a free sample blank postcard you can use write to:

**Rita DeLisi
Littlehouse
Box 141
Lindenhurst, NY 11757**

Chris Craven

WINDOW PAIN

Ask for a postcard and mention *SWAK*. (There's no telling what extra surprise Rita may send you.)

Tape or glue on a magazine or newspaper picture. The postcard maker changed this advertisement by drawing some extra makeup.

This girl has applied her make-up first incorrectly and then correctly.

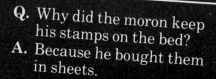

Q. Why did the moron keep his stamps on the bed?
A. Because he bought them in sheets.

When you find a picture you like printed on cardboard packaging (such as this cat from a cat food box) turn it into a postcard.

Put a store-bought postcard over the part of the picture you like most and trace around it. Cut it out, write "Post Card" on the back, and it's ready to use.

Stick on a decorative seal or magazine cutout, then make up the rest of the picture.

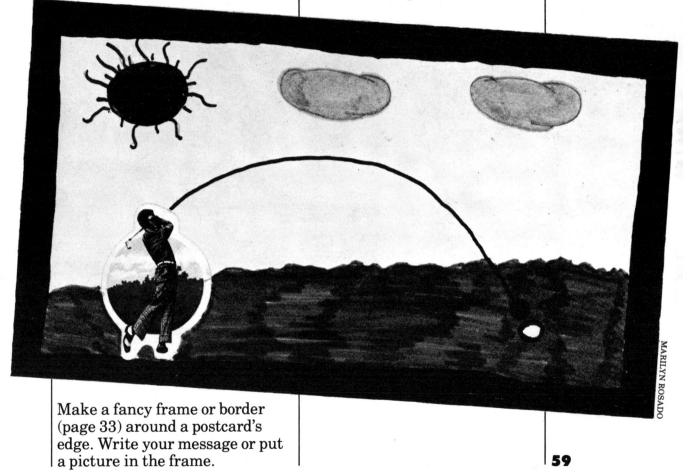

Make a fancy frame or border (page 33) around a postcard's edge. Write your message or put a picture in the frame.

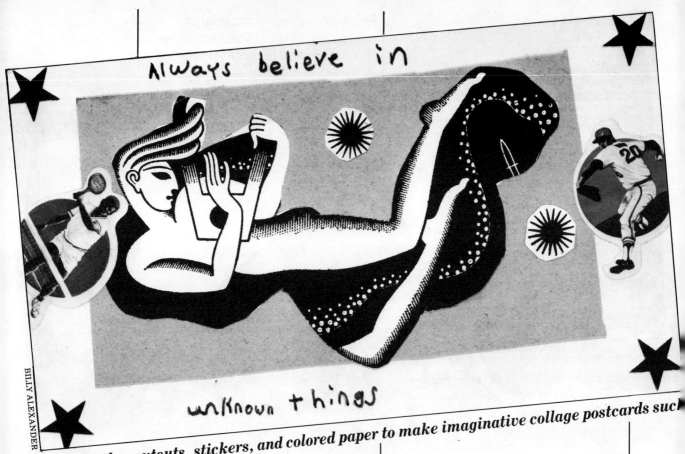

Always believe in unknown things

Put together cutouts, stickers, and colored paper to make imaginative collage postcards suc[h]
as this one.

Postcards or Postal Cards

The first postcards were plain paper cards imprinted with postage and sold by government postal systems. (Austria put out the first ones in 1869.) Picture postcards were made in Europe several years later.

In America, by law, only the government issued post-cards until the 1890s. Americans got their first look at European picture postcards at the World's Columbian Exposition of 1893 (a world's fair held in Chicago). They liked what they saw.

In 1898 the U.S. Congress allowed the printing of "Private Mailing Cards." Since these cards were not published by the government, the sender had to buy a postage stamp in order to mail the card. New postal regulations in 1901 required the words "POST CARD" to appear on the address side of privately-published picture postcards; from then on government-issued cards would be called "postal cards."

Things haven't changed much in 80 years: You can still buy plain postal cards with imprinted postage at any post office!

Tape or glue on a picture you made, or draw directly on a postcard.

Postcard Puzzles

One large picture can be cut into three or more postcards to make a kind of puzzle. The cards should be sent one after the other, on successive days, so the receiver gets one a day until he or she has all the pieces. The most surprising part of the whole picture should be the last card sent.

1. Start with a piece of cardboard or poster board 6 by 12 inches. (This makes three postcards 4 by 6 inches each.)

← 6-inches →

4-inches

12-inches

4-inches

4-inches

2. Measure carefully with a ruler, then draw the two lines where the three postcards will be cut apart.

3. Draw, paint, or color a large picture with some parts in each of the three sections. (Try to make each section interesting to look at by itself.)

4. After you finish the whole picture, cut the puzzle pieces apart.
5. Mail one each day for three days to the same person.

You can also put three postcards end to end to create a long puzzle like this one.

Personalize Store-Bought Postcards

Permanent markers work best on the shiny surfaces of most picture postcards. Add words (with or without cartoon balloons).

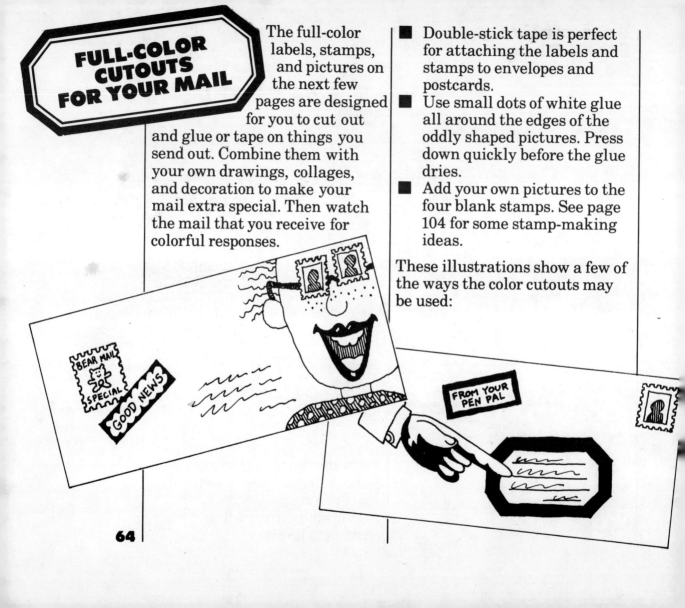

FULL-COLOR CUTOUTS FOR YOUR MAIL

The full-color labels, stamps, and pictures on the next few pages are designed for you to cut out and glue or tape on things you send out. Combine them with your own drawings, collages, and decoration to make your mail extra special. Then watch the mail that you receive for colorful responses.

■ Double-stick tape is perfect for attaching the labels and stamps to envelopes and postcards.

■ Use small dots of white glue all around the edges of the oddly shaped pictures. Press down quickly before the glue dries.

■ Add your own pictures to the four blank stamps. See page 104 for some stamp-making ideas.

These illustrations show a few of the ways the color cutouts may be used:

BEAR MAIL SPECIAL

GOOD NEWS

FROM YOUR PEN PAL

Celebrations

BIRTHDAY MAIL

One Birthday Cake to Go

This stand-up birthday card arrives flat in a standard envelope. The receiver connects the two ends with Scotch tape and (Ta-da!) he or she has a little paper cake—a "tasteful" reminder of your best wishes. (And you don't have to clean any pans!)

1. Cut out a rectangle of sturdy but not stiff paper (definitely not cardboard) slightly smaller than a standard 9-inch envelope. One factory-cut edge of the paper will be the bottom of the cake.
2. Draw a cake with fat candles similar to the one on this page. The tops of the candle flames should touch the top of the paper rectangle. Write the instructions at one end just as in the illustration.

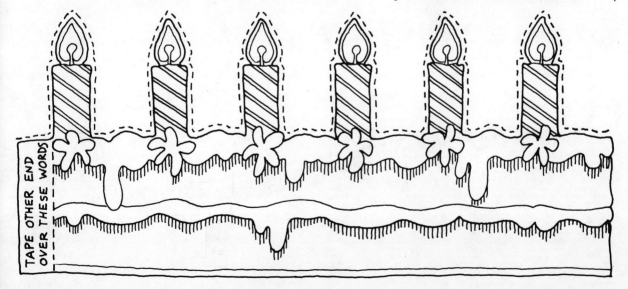

TAPE OTHER END OVER THESE WORDS

3. Draw a dotted line around the cake and candles. The friend you send it to can have the fun of cutting it out.
4. Decorate it with crayons or felt-tip pens.
5. Mail it in the envelope you used as a guide, and throw in some confetti or a real balloon.

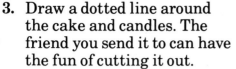

Other Stand-Up Cards

Folding a piece of sturdy paper one or more times will allow it to stand up by itself. Below are a few ways to fold paper to create interesting greeting cards. Use the factory-cut edge of the paper for a perfectly straight bottom. Cut around the outline of the top of your drawing to make the card more unusual.

Cards that Reach Out

Only the center of the birthday flower (left) is glued down to the card, leaving the fringelike petals free to be pulled forward when it is taken out of the envelope.

Parts that stick out (leaves on trees; arms, legs, and noses on funny characters; doors and window shutters on little buildings) make cards more fun. Cut the piece that will stick out from a separate sheet of paper, leaving a little extra as a tab. Use glue to attach the tab to the rest of the picture.

← Fringe hair

← Stick-out ears, nose, and tongue

Write messages behind shutters and doors →

*This is not a stamped envelope.
It's a card drawn by Marjorie Merena
who loves to create her own stamps and postmarks. The stamps spell
out the card's message (with the help of some happy little koalas).
The postmark contains the birthdate (February 13) of Marjorie's cat,
Anouk, for whom the card was made.*

BRIAN JONES

In Two Words or Less...

Thank you notes won't be a chore once you realize how few words are really necessary. Say it simply: Thank you.

A postcard is just right for a short message. Make the words decorative with fancy writing (see page 52).

If you're saying thanks for a gift that's easy to draw—draw it. Or cut its shape out of colored paper and write your message on the cutout. (Mail it in an envelope.)

Cut a music note out of stiff paper and write your message on it. This thank you *note* is specially suited to musical gifts like records and harmonicas.

If your family owns a camera that takes instant photographs, ask someone to snap a picture of you using your gift ... with a big smile on your face. Sending that snapshot will say thank you without any words at all.

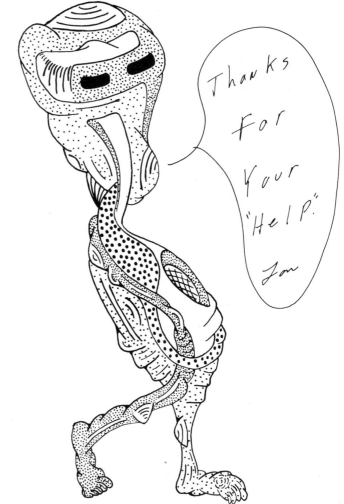

Lon Spiegelman (page 136) drew one of his fantastic creatures to say thank you.

Add a Heart and It's a Valentine

Store-bought postcards, snap-shots, magazine and newspaper pictures, advertisements, seed packets, and anything else that will fit in an envelope or turn into a postcard may become a valentine by the simple addition (and clever placement) of a heart-shaped sticker. You may write your own note on blank heart-shaped stickers, but the message will usually be clear even without words.

With a valentine message added, seed packets make great just-before-spring greetings, and fit easily in standard envelopes.

HERBS

PLANT HARTS SEEDS

SWEET BASIL

50¢ BASILICONE
BASILIC GRAND

ANNUAL
BASILICO

NET WT. 1.5 G

YOU'RE SWEET, VALENTINE

Purina® **Tender Vittles** cat food

A 100% nutritionally complete and balanced meal

Lots of little heart-shaped stickers were added to this cat food ad cut from a magazine. The bottom sticker was cut so that the cat's tongue appears to be in front of it.

75

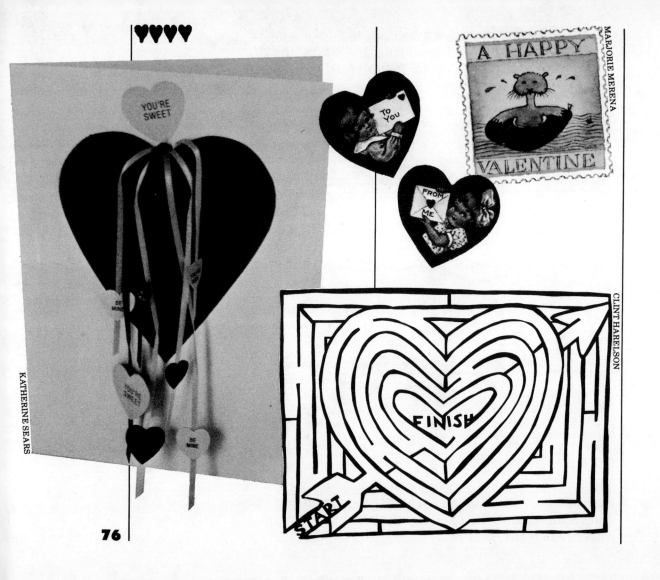

MARJORIE MERENA

CLINT HARELSON

KATHERINE SEARS

YOU'RE SWEET

BE MINE

YOU'RE SWEET

BE MINE

TO YOU

FROM ME

A HAPPY VALENTINE

FINISH

START

How to Cut Out a Heart

1. Fold a piece of paper in half.
2. Hold the fold with your non-scissor hand.

3. Lightly draw the shape of an ice cream cone on the paper.

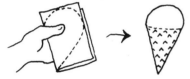

4. Cut out the shape.

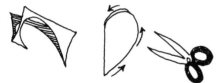

5. Open it up: it's a heart!

The Official Valentine Postmark

There's a very good reason for getting your valentines made and addressed early this year: if you have them ready to mail by February 5, your valentines can get the official valentine postmark and decoration from the "heart of America"—Valentine, Nebraska.

1. Address and stamp your valentine mail as usual.
2. Now put them together into a big envelope addressed to:
3. Include a note asking Mrs. Mulligan to please stamp your mail with the chamber of commerce logo.
4. Be sure to put enough postage on the big envelope.

When she gets them, Mrs. Mulligan will stamp your valentines with the "Heart City's" decorative logo and will then mail them from the town post office where they'll get postmarked VALENTINE, NE.

CHAMBER OF COMMERCE

VALENTINE, NEBRASKA

"THE HEART CITY"

VALENTINE, NE
MAR 10
PM
1981
69201

Judy Mulligan, Secretary
Chamber of Commerce
Valentine, NE 69201

Remember, they're being mailed twice, so if they are to get to your friends by February 14 you must mail your stamped and addressed valentines to the chamber of commerce by February 5.

Stamped with a Kiss

As a special treat for *SWAK* readers (that's you!) Karen Richards, president of Inkadinkado, has created a rubber stamp that will help you seal every piece of mail beautifully . . . with a kiss.

You can get this rubber stamp, instructions for creating a handle for it from a sewing thread spool, some of Karen's famous rubber stamp secrets, and a mini-catalog of some other great stamps; just send your request along with 25¢ and a SASE to:

**SWAK Rubber Stamp
Inkadinkado
95 Prince St.
Jamaica Plain, MA 02130**

Loving Messages

These messages aren't just for valentines. Use them all year round.

I Love You

Sealed With A Kiss

Sealed With A Kiss For Every Mile Between Us

Sealed With Oceans And Oceans Of Love With A Kiss On Every Wave

Sealed With A Lick 'Cause A Kiss Wouldn't Stick

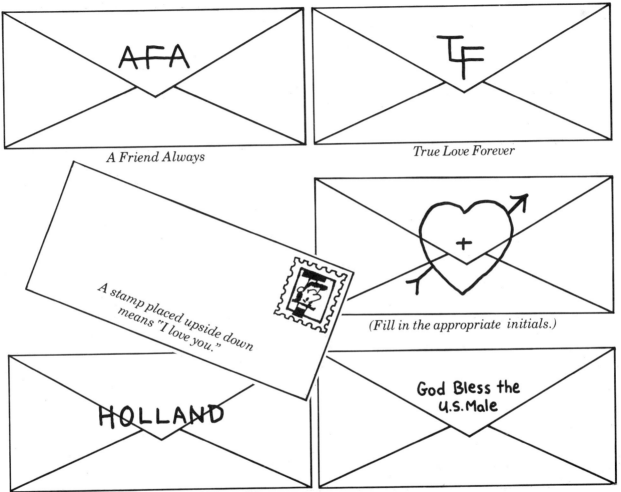

AFA

A Friend Always

TF

True Love Forever

A stamp placed upside down means "I love you."

(Fill in the appropriate initials.)

HOLLAND

Hope Our Love Lasts And Never Dies

God Bless the U.S. Male

Send a Mask Through the Mail

A postcard mask may be the most unusual Halloween card your friends will ever receive.

1. Cut out a 4-by-6-inch postcard from a piece of cardboard.
2. With a ruler, draw diagonal lines from corner to corner. The place where the lines cross each other is the center of the card.
3. Measure 1¼ inches to each side of the center point and punch holes there with the tips of your scissors. Neatly cut out eyeholes about this size:

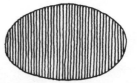

4. Cut a nose slit small enough so that it will hold onto your nose and keep the mask on your face. (Look, Ma, no hands!)
5. Decorate the mask with colored paper, paint, crayons, or markers.
6. Write your friend's name and address on the back of the mask and mail it with a first-class stamp.

Jack·O·Lantern

LOUISIANA
YAMS
SWEET POTATO PIECES IN SYRUP

NET WEIGHT 29 OZ. (1 LB. 13 OZ.)

Jack·O·Lantern

10/72

CLINT,
I YAM
HOPING YOU
WILL HAVE A
HAPPY
HALLOWEEN!

LOVE,
TRUDY

TRUDY DeCANIO

Can labels can become funny, fabulous greeting cards. The artist chose this one for Halloween because of the brand name, then drew pumpkin faces on the yams and pasted on a holiday message.

MARGO EGLIN

Symmetrical Cutouts

1. Fold a small rectangular piece of paper in half.
2. Draw one-half of a picture/design.
3. Cut out the design, then cut holes for eyes, nose, mouth, and decorations.
4. Open up to see the whole design.

83

Halloween Alphabet

Redraw one of these as the initial letter of a friend's name on a Halloween envelope, or put them together to create fancy-looking words. Make up your own picture A-B-C's for decorating mail for other holidays.

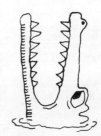

Christmas: Time to Recycle

With a little forethought and imagination the Christmas cards your family received last year can become the cards you send this year.

TRUDY DeCANIO

Put the cards in a safe place. Some you may want to save forever, others are fun to recycle. Use the front of a card to make a postcard. Cut it apart at the fold. Write "Post Card" on the back of the piece with the picture, and draw a line down the center. Send it as a Christmas postcard with your own message written on the left.

Some cards have pictures that can be cut out and made into tree trimmings. Punch a hole near the top, put a colored string or ribbon through it, and tie a knot. Write your message on the back, then mail the cutout ornament in an envelope.

Begin a tradition with a close friend by sending him or her the same card he sent *you* last year. Write your name and this year's date beneath his signature. Each Christmas the card will be at one or the other's house. Some people end up sending the same card back and forth for years.

A Family Newspaper

Make a one-page "newspaper" full of family highlights of the past year to send friends and relatives. Another member of your family might enjoy working on this with you, so ask.

1. Think up a name for your paper (The Thompson Times, Harrison Hotline, Garcia Gazette) and put it at the top of a sheet of typing paper. Write in black ink.
2. Type or print short descriptions of family happenings: new jobs, hobbies, trips, sports, school news, and so forth.
3. Find a clear family snapshot to tape on.
4. Add a holiday greeting.
5. After you've finished making the original, have copies made on an instant copier.
6. Fold each copy in three parts and staple or seal with a sticker. There's no need for an envelope—just put stamp and the address the back.

Eight Cards for the Festival of Lights

Chanukah is an eight-day December holiday; why not send eight greetings so that one arrives each day? Make eight simple postcards, each bearing one of the letters of the holiday's name:

Make each letter big and colorful, and decorate the cards with candles, dreidels, and other holiday images. Send them in correct order (or mix them up if you prefer to make it a puzzle), one each day.

A Christmas Postmark Collection

North Pole, AK
99705
Holy City, CA
95026
Bethlehem, CT
06751
Christmas, FL
32709
Santa Claus, IN
47579
Mistletoe, KY
41351

Noel, MO
64854
Christmas
Valley, OR
97638
Snow, OK
74567
Snow Shoe, PA
16874
Snowflake, VA
24251

For more on postmark collecting see page 106.

Between December 1 and December 26, 1979, the United States Postal Service delivered over 8½ billion pieces of mail. And you thought Santa had a lot to do!! To avoid the rush this year, mail your holiday greetings early in December.

On the Back

When you make your own greeting cards and postcards, let people know it. Make up a name for your very own card company with slogan, logo, and all, and put it on the back of each card you make. For example:

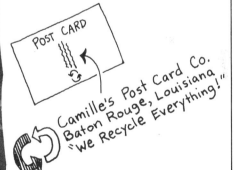

When You Care Enough

To Send the Very Cheapest!
A NANCY MOOREHEAD ORIGINAL...
(greeting cards plus)

POST CARD

Camille's Post Card Co.
Baton Rouge, Louisiana
"We Recycle Everything!"

Look at what's written on the back of store-bought cards for idea starters.

89

Enclose a little extra something in a letter to make your mail more fun. Make, find, or buy small, flat, unbreakable things that fit in an envelope. Write "Please Hand Cancel" on the front of the envelope near the stamp.

A COLLECTION FOR BEGINNERS

WOODEN NICKEL
UNITED STATES OF AMERICA

Collections

Ever since Britain printed the first adhesive postage stamp 140 years ago, stamps have become perhaps the most collected collectibles in the world. In the United States alone over 20 million people collect stamps.

The World's Most Popular Hobby

Stamp collecting, also called "philately," is a natural for anyone who loves sending and receiving mail. If you save letters in their envelopes and the postcards you get, you already have a beginning stamp collection. Keep them in a shoe box or a convenient drawer. Ask friends, neighbors, and even your school secretary to save envelopes for you—especially any that come from other countries. If either your dad or mom works in an office, he or she may be able to watch for unusual stamps that arrive there.

Saving stamps at random creates a general collection. Look through your envelopes to see what interests you most. Do you prefer stamps of your own country or ones from foreign lands? Stamps with pictures on a particular theme, like sports or animals, may appeal to you. You may even decide to collect unofficial stamps like Christmas Seals used on holiday mail. Philatelists (stamp collectors) may choose to study and collect any aspect of postage that interests them.

92

Collecting United Nations Stamps

United Nations stamps are unique. They are the only accepted postage stamps not issued by a country but by an international organization, and they can only be used on mail sent from U.N. headquarters in New York City or Geneva (Switzerland). The stamps are beautifully designed by artists from all over the world. Write for the free booklet, *Introductory Guide to United Nations Stamps*, and an order form. This full-color booklet shows lots of stamps and tells about all the philatelic items you can collect.

Your booklet will arrive in an envelope bearing a U.N. stamp and postmark — the first for your collection!

Collecting Canadian Stamps

If Canadian stamps are your interest, write for the free booklet, *The Joys of Stamp Collecting*. It contains good information for beginners, collecting hints, and a glossary of terms.

Don't forget to ask for the booklet by name and include your return address.

Canada Post
Public Affairs Branch
Sir Alex Campbell Bldg.
Confederation Heights
Ottawa, ON
K1A 0B1

U.N. Postal Admin.
P.O. Box 5900,
Grand Central Sta.
New York, NY 10017

Types of Stamps

Airmail stamps are now only necessary on mail that is flown overseas. At one time airmail was a separate and faster class of mail within the U.S.

Regular postage stamps (also called "definitives") are small stamps with simple designs.

Special-purpose stamps indicate a special type of service paid for; for instance, special delivery.

Commemorative stamps honor special people or subjects or celebrate historic events. They are usually larger and more colorful than regular stamps and are on sale for a shorter period of time.

Postage-due stamps are put on mail at the post office to show that not enough postage was used on a letter. The "postage due" is usually paid at the letter's destination by its receiver.

Only commemorative, current regular, and special-purpose stamps, and postal stationery (pre-stamped postal cards, envelopes, and aerogrammes) are sold by the USPS and Canada Post. (Older and foreign stamps may be purchased from a local dealer, hobby shop, or mail-order stamp company.) Both countries offer special services for collectors. You can find out what stamps and services are currently available by writing:

**United States
  Postal Service
Philatelic Sales Branch
Washington, DC 20265**

**Philatelic Service
Canada Post Office
Ottawa, ON
K1A 0B5**

More! More!

Information about stamps is easy to find. Look under "postage stamps" in your public library. Also, your library may subscribe to some of the magazines and newspapers on the subject—*Linn's Stamp News, Minkus Stamp Journal, Scott Monthly Journal, Scottalk,* and *Stamps.* Look in the Yellow Pages under "Stamps for Collectors" for a listing of stamp dealers in your area.

In a current stamp catalog you can find out all about a stamp—its country, date of issue, current value, and more. Find its picture in the catalog and you'll find the information you're after. (Stamp catalogs also can be found in your public library.)

Hobby Helps and Hints

- There's no need to buy a stamp album to begin collecting. Keep your stamps filed carefully in envelopes. Once you decide on the type of collection you would like, buy a suitable album—or make your own. A loose-leaf notebook with graph-paper pages makes an excellent album. The graph paper makes it easy to keep your stamps evenly spaced.

- Always handle stamps carefully. They are small and delicate, and can easily be soiled or torn. Experienced stamp collectors use tongs to pick up, examine, and move stamps; not being handled by fingers keeps stamps clean.

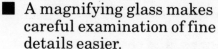

- A magnifying glass makes careful examination of fine details easier.

- When mounting stamps in an album, never use glue, paste, or tape. Use clear acetate mounts or inexpensive stamp hinges.

  1. Fold the hinge, gummed side out, about one-third from the end.
  2. First moisten this part and attach to back of stamp.

  3. Next moisten this part and attach to album page.

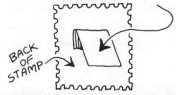

BACK OF STAMP

When dry, stamps can be peeled away from stamp hinges without damage.

Stamps on Approval

Many philatelists find that the easiest way to buy stamps is through the mail from one of many excellent mail-order stamp companies. The companies have developed a service called "stamps on approval" which allows you to examine stamps for a short time before you buy them.

If you write to say you're interested, the stamp dealer sends you about a dozen little envelopes filled with interesting stamps of different kinds. Each envelope is printed with information about the stamps and the price of the selection.

You may examine the stamps for 10 days, usually, and select the ones you want to buy for your collection. Put the stamps you do *not* want in an envelope along with payment for the ones you are keeping, and send it back to the company. You may return all the stamps if you wish—there's no obligation to buy.

After you return the first selection, the company will prepare and send a different selection of stamps for your approval. Of course, you may cancel the service at any time and no more stamps will be sent.

Following are offers from three approval stamp dealers. Write for only *one* of the offers (you avoid confusion by dealing with only one company at a time). Remember: stamps on approval is a way of *buying* stamps. Only use it if you have money to spend on building your collection.

Fifty Different U.S. Stamps

Globus Stamp Co. specializes in U.S. stamps, so if you're building a U.S. collection their approval selections may be just right for you.

Globus offers 50 different U.S. stamps that you can keep for only 25¢. Send your full name and address, one quarter, and your request for *50 Different U.S. Stamps* to:

One Thousand Stamps for $2.95

Kenmore Stamp Co. offers a tremendous selection of stamps from all over the world. As a special offer you can buy one thousand stamps for only $2.95. They're old and new, U.S., Canadian and foreign, and all different.

Send $2.95 in check or money order, your full name and address, and your request for one thousand stamps to:

**Globus Stamp Co.
Dept. BK-3
Box 727
Newton, IA 50208**

**Kenmore Stamp Co.
Milford, NH 03055**

Stamps on approval will be sent automatically with these offers.

Stamp Finder

Sometimes identifying the country a stamp comes from can be difficult. (Would you know that a stamp marked "Helvetia" comes from Switzerland?)

H. E. Harris & Co. is offering its excellent *Stamp Finder* free to beginning collectors to help identify foreign stamps. This little booklet contains foreign names, a collector's dictionary, and philatelic hints.

Q. What kind of stamp is the tastiest?
A. One in mint condition.

Ask for the *Stamp Finder* and Harris's *Get-Acquainted Catalog* (listing stamps, supplies, and unusual items like *Star Wars* seals and other gummed stickers). If you'd like to receive stamps on approval, say so; otherwise none will be sent. Remember to include your full name, address, and ZIP code.

H. E. Harris & Co., Inc.
Dept. SWAK
Boston, MA 02117

H. E. Harris & Co., the world's largest stamp firm, began as a mail-order stamp business owned and run by 14-year-old Henry Ellis Harris in 1916. Henry's office was his bedroom.

Join the Club!

Once you get into philately, you'll probably want to join a stamp club. Through a club you can share your interest with other people, meet fellow collectors, ask questions, gain knowledge, and swap, buy, and sell stamps. You have a choice of several different kinds of clubs:

1. A school club, such as the Benjamin Franklin Stamp Club.

2. A local club. Check with your public library for the names and phone numbers of local stamp clubs. Such clubs usually have members of all ages, monthly meetings, and lots of opportunities for you to see more experienced philatelists' collections firsthand.

3. A national stamp club such as the Junior Philatelists of America. The JPA is a national stamp society run by and for young people (up to age 22). Members act as officers, write for the club's

journal—*Philatelic Observer*, serve in study groups, and operate such services as a pen pal department, stamp exchange program, stamp identification and first-day cover service. For more information, a membership application, and a free copy of *Philatelic Observer*, send your request, full name and address, and two first-class stamps (a SASE isn't necessary) to:

**Junior Philatelists of America
Central Office
Box 383
Boonville, NY 13309**

4. A topical club (see page 102).

1981   **Philadelphia, PA**

colonial-theme post office in a building once owned by Ben. You can get a souvenir postmark from this post office by following the instructions on page 107 in the section titled Go!

Self-addressed postal card

**Postmaster
B. Free Franklin Post Office
316 Market St.
Philadelphia, PA 19106**

VIP

Ben Franklin is about the most important person in the history of the North American postal service. He was the first postmaster general of the U.S. and the Father of the Canada Post Office. In 1847, after his death, his picture appeared on the first U.S. postage stamp.

In Philadelphia there is a

Be sure to ask your teacher about starting a Ben Franklin Stamp Club in your school. The local post office will be happy to give her the information.

Birds and butterflies*

Collecting by Topic

Topical stamp collecting stresses the designs on stamps. Here are a few of the hundreds of topics that can be found pictured on them (an entire collection could be built around any one):

Flowers*

Sports

Flags*

Aviation

Animals*

Royalty

Art*

Mythology

Space*

*The USPS sells stamp collecting kits on these topics. Each one contains genuine postage stamps, a 20-page album, mounting hinges, and a beginner's stamp collecting booklet. They're available at most post offices for $2 apiece.

There are dozens of topical clubs through which people with similar collecting interests get together. Here are five that welcome kids and may be especially interesting to you:

Karen Cartier
ATA Fairy-Tale/Folklore
   Study Unit
2509 Buffalo Dr.
Arlington, TX 76013

Vaughn H. Augustin
Christmas Philatelic Club
P.O. Box 77
Scottsbluff, NE 69361

Jewell Sonderegger
Fine Arts Philatelists
P.O. Box 1606
Midland, MI 48640

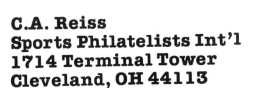

C.A. Reiss
Sports Philatelists Int'l
1714 Terminal Tower
Cleveland, OH 44113

William P. York
Int'l Association
   of Space Philatelists
P.O. Box 302
Yonkers, NY 10710

HOMEMADE STAMPS

ROSE AVERY

NO NUKES POSTAGE New York

LON SPIEGELMAN

MICHAEL SCOTT

WORK OF ART BY JAS. W. FELTER

1974 Canadada

Homemade stamps are just for fun. They decorate mail and delight your correspondents, but you still have to buy official stamps for postage.

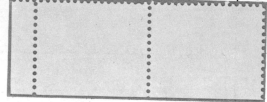

When you buy commemorative stamps, ask the postal clerk for the *selvage*, the blank paper at the edge of the stamp sheet. The selvage has gum on the back too, and since the front is blank you can draw on whatever images you like to create your own stamps.

Another way to make decorative stamps is to cut small pictures from out-of-date magazines. Pinking shears give a zigzag stamplike edge. If you cut with regular scissors, draw a stamplike edge around the picture.

How about stamps with your own picture on them? Xerox a whole sheet of your school pictures before you cut them apart. Make the copy look like a sheet of stamps by adding the name of an imaginary postal system (Bobmail, for example), stamp prices, and color with felt-tip pen.

If your family owns a sewing machine, it can be used to perforate sheets of homemade stamps. Ask the person most familiar with the machine to *remove the thread* and carefully push the paper through, guiding the needle between the rows of "stamps."

E.F. HIGGINS III

HARLEY FRANCIS

ROSE AVERY

Use glue or double-stick tape to attach your homemade stamps to mail.

On Your Marks...

A postmark is the official impression stamped on a piece of mail to show the place and date of cancellation.

COLLECT POSTMARKS

The "town circle" shows the date of cancellation and the name of the post office where the impression was made. The "kill bars," or "killer," mark the adhesive stamp to show it has been used.

Get Set...

You don't need any special tools or materials for collecting postmarks. (However, the general hints on storing a collection, on page 114, also apply here.) You do need to know about the USPS's *National ZIP Code and Post Office Directory.* This big book contains (in alphabetical order) the names and ZIP codes of almost all the post offices in the United States. Use the *Directory* for finding the names and ZIP codes of post offices whose postmarks you want to collect. Every post office and almost every library has a copy of the *Directory* for you to use. If you really take up postmark collecting as a hobby you can buy your own copy from your local post office. It costs $8.

Go!

Begin by saving all the postmarks on mail that comes to your house. Postmarks that arrive by chance may give you ideas for more specialized collections. For example, if you happened to find a postmark from Turkey, Kentucky, you might decide to collect marks with bird names. If you discovered your collection already contained marks from many post offices in your own state, you might try to get one from *every* office in your state (a big project!).

Once you have an idea for a specific kind of collection, you can actually "order" postmarks for it. Here's how:

1. Find the name and ZIP code of a post office whose mark you want in the *National ZIP Code and Post Office Directory.*
2. Address a pre-stamped postal card to yourself.

3. On a separate piece of paper write a note something like this:

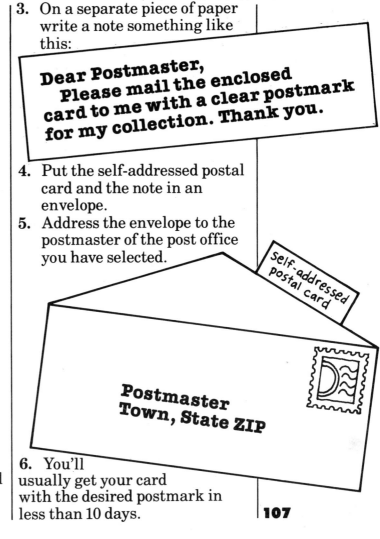

Dear Postmaster,
Please mail the enclosed card to me with a clear postmark for my collection. Thank you.

4. Put the self-addressed postal card and the note in an envelope.
5. Address the envelope to the postmaster of the post office you have selected.

Self-addressed postal card

Postmaster
Town, State ZIP

6. You'll usually get your card with the desired postmark in less than 10 days.

Collecting for Kicks

Many post offices in America have unusual—often funny—names, and some folks specialize in collecting their postmarks. Consider a card from Bigfoot (Bigfoot, TX 78005, that is!) or from Dinosaur (Dinosaur, CO 81610). Below are the names of some other post offices whose postmarks you might enjoy collecting.

Bat Cave,
NC 28710

Boring, OR
97009

Eek, AK
99578

Eureka, SD
57437

Loveland, CO
80537

Mouthcard,
KY 41548

Riddle, OR
97469

Rough &
Ready, CA
95975

Sandwich, IL
60548

Tarzan, TX
79783

Uncle Sam, LA
70792

Volcano, HI
96785

Worlds of Fun,
MO 64108

Zap, ND
58580

The Friendliest Club in the World . . .

That's what director Jay W. Lounsbury calls the Post Mark Collectors Club (PMCC). If ZIP code games and post offices with funny names tickle your fancy, the Post Mark Collectors Club may be just for you. Membership for junior members is $3 and includes a year's subscription to the PMCC *Bulletin*, plenty of free postmarks, and lots of collecting help and advice. Send a SASE for a free information sheet and application, a sample *Bulletin*, and some postmarks.

Postmarks from Outer Space

(or Mail from Mars with the Postmark to Prove It)

Cosmos, MN 56228	Mars, PA 16046
Earth, TX 79031	Moon, KY 41457
Enterprise, UT 84725	Neptune, NJ 07753
Jupiter, FL 33458	Stars, MS 39167
	Sun, LA 70463
	Sunspot, NM 88349
	Venus, FL 33960

Jay W. Lounsbury
Post Mark Collectors Club
2508 Lakehurst Ave.
Forestville, MD 20028

A Friendship Collection

Why not make a collection of postmarks with the names of your friends. Many given names are listed below. If you don't find the names you are looking for there, look them up in the *National ZIP Code and Post Office Directory*.

Do you have a friend named . . .

Monroe, VA 24574

Florence, MT 59833

Elizabeth, LA 70638
Elliot, MD 21823
Emily, MN 56447
Erin, TN 37061

Troy, SC 29848

Elsie, NE 69134

Albert, TX 78601
Alfred, ME 04002
Alice, ND 58003
Allen, AL 36419
Alma, OK 73003
Angela, MT 59312
Anita, PA 15711
Anna, OH 45302
Annette, AK 99920
Arthur, TN 37707
Barrett, WV 25013
Barry, MN 56210
Bart, PA 17503
Bessie, OK 73622
Beverly, WA 99321
Bill, WY 82631
Bonnie, IL 62816
Brent, FL 32503
Bruce, SD 57220
Burt, NY 14028
Carl, GA 30203
Carlos, MN 56319
Caroline, WI 54928
Cary, NC 27511
Cass, WV 24927
Cayce, SC 29033
Charlotte, IA 52731

Chloe, WV 25235
Christopher, IL 62822
Clifford, IN 47226
Clint, TX 79836
Cody, WY 82414
Constance, KY 41009
Craig, MO 64437
Daisy, OK 74540
Dale, NY 14039
Daniel, WY 83115
David, KY 41616
Dennis, MS 38838
Donna, TX 78537
Dorothy, NJ 08317
Douglas, AZ 85607
Duncan, SC 29334
Dusty, NM 87934

Edward, NC 27821

Floyd, NM 88118
Frank, WV 24937
Gail, TX 79738
Glen, NH 03838
Gordon, GA 31031
Grace, ID 83241
Greer, AZ 85927
Gregory, NC 27940
Guy, TX 77444
Helen, MD 20635
Henry, VA 24102
Hope, RI 02831
Imogene, IA 51645
Ina, IL 62846
Jack, AL 36346
Jacob, IL 62950
Jane, MO 64846
Jay, NY 12941
Jean, NV 89019
Jeannette, PA 15644
Jennie, AR 71649
Jerome, AR 71650
Jessie, ND 58452
Joanna, SC 29351
Joseph, UT 84739
Joshua, TX 76058
Joyce, WA 98343
Juanita, ND 58453
Juliette, GA 31046
Katherine, AZ 86430
Kathleen, FL 33849
Keith, KY 40846
Kelly, WY 83011
Kent, CT 06757
Kermit, TX 79745

Kevin, MT 59454
Kim, CO 81049
Kirk, CO 80824
Laura, OH 45337
Laurel, VA 23060
Lee, OH 44120
Leroy, AL 36548
Leslie, MI 49251
Libby, MT 59923
Lindsey, PA 15767
Luke, MD 21540
Lulu, FL 32061
Lynn, AR 72440
Mack, CO 81525
Mark, IL 61340
Martha, OK 73556
Martin, MI 49070
Mary, KY 41350
Matthew, KY 41454
Melissa, TX 75071
Michael, IL 62065
Milton, TN 37118
Mina, NV 89422
Mona, UT 84645
Morris, CT 06763
Norma, NJ 08347
Norman, IN 47264
Otis, OR 97368
Paul, AL 36469
Pedro, OH 45659
Ralph, SD 57650
Randolph, TX 75475
Ray, IN 46737
Rebecca, GA 31783
Reva, SD 57651
Rich, MS 38662
Robert, LA 70455
Rocky, OK 73661

Rodney, MI 49342
Roland, IA 50236
Rose, NE 68772
Ross, ND 58776
Roy, WA 98580
Rufus, OR 97050
Russell, NY 13684
Ruth, MS 39662
Sandy, UT 84070
Sarah, MS 38665

Saul, KY 40981
Scott, MS 38772
Shannon, NC 28386
Sharon, MA 02067
Shirley, NY 11967
Sidney, AR 72577
Stacy, MN 55079
Stephen, MN 56757
Stuart, NE 68780
Susan, VA 23163

Sylvia, KS 67581
Terry, MS 39170
Theresa, WI 53091
Tina, MO 64682
Todd, PA 16685
Tony, WI 54563
Tracy, MN 56175
Troy, ID 83871
Van, KY 41857
Viola, DE 19979

Virginia, IL 62691
Vivian, LA 71082
Wanda, MN 56294
Warren, OR 97053
Wayne, NE 68787
Wendell, MA 01379
Winn, ME 04495
Woody, CA 93287
Zachariah, KY 41396
Zoe, KY 41397

CYNDY HARRY

GREETINGS FROM GRAND CANYON ARIZ.

POSTCARD CRAZY

Picture postcards were first printed in Europe in the 1870s. By the turn of the century the idea had really caught on — especially with travelers who wanted to show the folks back home the colorful, exciting places they were visiting — and soon there was a postcard craze. In Europe and America, people kept albums filled with cards to show to all their guests.

Postcards were inexpensive, entertaining, exotic, and romantic.

Perhaps your grandparents have saved one of those old collections as a family keepsake, or at least have saved a few cards for special reasons. Be careful with them for they may be valuable family mementos.

The only thing more amazing than the number of postcards printed in the past 80 years (millions upon millions) is the variety of those cards. Almost every recreational and historic site, public building, and monument has shown up on a postcard at one time or another. (Supposedly, the best-selling postcard in the world pictures the White House in Washington, D.C.)

Natural wonders, beaches, and vacation spots are very popular. But postcards also show art, cartoons, trick photography (like a Texan riding a giant jackrabbit), maps, animals, people, words and names, puzzles, holidays, vehicles, disasters, and monsters—you name it!

Almost anything you're interested in can be found pictured on postcards.

Deltiology

"Deltiology" is the fancy word for postcard collecting. If you're a collector, you're a "deltiologist." Start a collection by saving every picture postcard that comes your way—new or old,

photograph or art reproduction, color or black-and-white, printed or handmade. Later, when you've decided which ones you like most, you can trade the others with fellow deltiologists.

Store your cards in a shoe box. If you wish to organize them by category, make cardboard dividers a little taller than your postcards and write the category name at the top of each one. Put a divider in front of the cards in each category.

Postcard albums of various sorts and prices are available at hobby shops. Some, with plastic pages, allow you to view both sides of a card without removing it.

The condition of cards is important. The fresher and cleaner they are, the more valuable.

113

Keep your most special cards in plastic or waxed paper sandwich bags or glassine envelopes.

The postmark and stamp on a used card may tell collectors the date of that card, and may also double its collection value. And as a bonus, used cards have the added interest of a written message.

Sometimes you'll find old cards that were never used (they are in mint condition). Their good condition will add to the beauty of your collection. Some folks like to buy inexpensive mint cards to send as greetings; they're sometimes cheaper and often more interesting than new ones.

General Collection Hints

The following suggestions apply to postcard, stamp, and autograph collecting.

■ Never make any marks on a collectible.

■ Never use glue, paste, or tape for mounting. Adhesives cause damage. Use peelable hinges, mounting corners, or plastic sleeves.

■ Never use scissors on a collectible. Trimming may destroy its value.

■ When making a display, never put tacks or staples through an object. Even tiny holes may reduce its value.

■ Store items flat. Never fold.

■ Store in a clean, dry place between unprinted paper or plastic sheets.

■ Try to keep your collectibles in their best possible condition.

Collect Antique Picture Postcards

One of the largest postcard clubs in the world (about two thousand members) is Deltiologists of America. If you are interested in collecting very old postcards, write for their excellent publication, *Deltiology, Special Invitation Edition*, a six-page folder containing beginner's collecting information, postcard illustrations, club membership rates, and an application form. You must send a 9-inch SASE to receive this publication.

SASE

**Deltiologists of America
3709 Gradyville Rd.
Newtown Square, PA 19073**

Where the Cards Are

They're everywhere! Just look around your house and you're likely to find half a dozen tucked in drawers and other places.

For old cards check in junk stores, antique shops, and at flea markets, and attend local postcard club shows.

New postcards are sold in many different places. Art museums and galleries have large selections of art reproduction cards (and nowadays some artists are creating art especially for postcards). Science museums sell exciting cards with pictures of dinosaurs, rockets, and outer space. Tourist centers and historic sites almost always sell their own postcards.

Many businesses—restaurants, hotels, motels, and tourist centers—give away free cards. Keep your eyes open for giveaways, especially when you travel.

Stamp Out Postcard Collecting!

If you're a deltiologist or a postmark collector, Herb Harrington (who's been a collector ever since he was a Cub Scout) makes rubber stamps to help you spread the word. Advertise your hobby by stamping all your correspondence with one of the stamps pictured to the left.

For one rubber stamp send 50¢ and a SASE with two first-class stamps to:

Herb Harrington
P. O. Box 585
Vienna, OH 44473

Find Fellow Postcard Fans

One of the best ways for a serious collector to find cards and increase his or her knowledge of the hobby is to join a club.

For the name of a postcard club near you call your public library or write to:

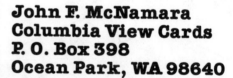

John F. McNamara
Columbia View Cards
P. O. Box 398
Ocean Park, WA 98640

John is a very friendly and helpful deltiologist. Be sure to tell him about your interest in postcards — what you collect, how long you've been collecting, and so forth.

Remember to enclose a SASE.

Heroic Postcards

Jackie Leventhal, also known as "the rubber stamp lady," is a mail artist who makes her living creating and selling postcards and rubber stamps. She runs a company called Hero Arts. Jackie's heroic postcards are weird and funny, and would be a fine addition to any deltiologist's collection. She'll send you one free if you send a SASE. You'll also get a sheet showing all her postcard designs with details of how to order the ones you like most (35¢ each). Send a SASE and your request for a free postcard to:

A rubber stamp catalog from Hero Arts is only $1 if you mention *SWAK* when ordering it. Jackie says even if you don't order stamps the catalog is full of great pictures and cartoons to cut out and use on your mail art.

By the way, Hero Arts sends a free rubber stamp to the artist who sends the most original piece of mail art each month, so get to work and make Jackie a postcard. After all, she's sending you one; that's what mail art is all about!

SASE

Jackie Leventhal
Hero Arts
P. O. Box 5234
Berkeley, CA 94705

Women's History on Cards

To name the company they began in 1973, Jocelyn Helaine Cohen and Nancy Victoria Taylor Poore combined their middle names: Helaine Victoria Press was born. Their catalog contains well over a hundred postcards (plus bookplates, notepaper, and posters) most of which picture important women in history and contain fascinating facts about their lives. Susan B. Anthony, Isadora Duncan, Amelia Earhart, Mother Jones, Kimura Komako (on this page), and many others appear on Helaine Victoria cards.

Nancy and Jocelyn do all the work at H.V. Press. They research history, design the postcards, print them on an 80-year-old cast iron letterpress, and correspond with their many customers.

Their cards are wonderful. To get one free, plus a catalog send two first-class stamps, your full name and address, and your request to:

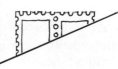

**Helaine Victoria Press
4080 Dynasty La.
Martinsville, IN 46151**

If you have a favorite woman in history or someone you'd like to know more about, say so in your letter.

Ken Brown's Crazy Cards

Ken Brown was a deltiologist long before he ever thought of making postcards. When he combined his hobby with his interest in photography and printed photos on Kodak postcard paper, his friends liked the results so much they were soon asking to buy his cards for themselves.

Before he knew it, Ken was in business. Being a cartoonist and animated-film maker, he also started drawing cartoon postcards like the one on this page besides making color postcards from photographs he took on his travels across America.

Nowadays his cards are sold in shops all over America, and in France, Japan, and Holland. Ken says it's great to be in a business in which you get a lot of mail. Customers and fellow mail artists send him postcards all the time.

Ken will send you one of his crazy cards for the asking. Just send your full name and address, one first-class stamp, and your request to:

Ken Brown
65 Inman St.
Cambridge, MA 02139

People
to Write

There's a special thrill in corresponding with a pen pal far away where customs and holidays and even climate are different from your own. The surprise of stamps and postmarks you've never seen arriving on exotic looking stationery, the fun of learning about another country firsthand from someone your own age, and the joy of building a new friendship based on similar interests all make pen pal correspondence an exciting experience.

Of course, a pen pal doesn't have to live in a foreign land. You can have fun and learn more about your own country through a correspondence with someone in a different part of the U.S. or Canada.

Sometimes pen friendships last for years and correspondents eventually exchange visits as well as letters.

Get a Pen Pal

What follows is a list of organizations that will give you the name and address of a pen pal in a foreign country or another state. Read about each group to find the one that's right for you, then write for a registration form and further information.

If you want to speed up the process of getting your pen pal, follow these directions carefully:

1. Write a letter to your chosen organization including your full name, address, age, date of birth, sex, and hobbies or interests. If you can speak or write a foreign language, say so.
2. Enclose the required money.
3. Enclose a SASE if requested.

If you're 11 to 17 years old and would like a friend in Africa or Asia, write to the Afro-Asian Pen Pal Center.

The International Cultural Center for Youth in Jerusalem will match you with an Israeli pen pal aged 12 to 18. There's no charge, but please, to cover return postage, send an international reply coupon along with your request.

Afro-Asian Pen Pal Center
C.P.O. Box 871
Kingston, NY 12401

Once you get the form it will cost you 70¢ for each name desired. Director Robert Carroll will also send along his excellent *Helpful Tips for Good Letter Writing to Africa and Asia.*

If you're a Boy Scout, write for information about free pen pals to:

I.C.C.Y.
Pen Pals
P.O. Box 8009
Jerusalem, Israel

Remember to use airmail stamps on all correspondence overseas.

Boy Scouts of America
Int'l Letter Exchange
P.O. Box 61030
Dallas/Fort Worth Airport,
TX 75261

The International Friendship League has gotten more than three million pen pals together since it began in 1946; today its members cover 130 countries around the world. If you're between 7 and 18 years old, $3 will get you a life membership and as many pen pals as you can keep up with. Send a SASE for a registration form to:

Most pen pals correspond in English, but if you're learning another language, receiving a letter in that language can be great fun. International Pen Friends offers its service in English, French, German, and Spanish. (You may also write for information about service in other languages.) IPF also has a stamp exchange division and provides international contacts for blind people.

The dues are $4 for the first year. You receive a list of possible pen pals and the club newsletter. IPF's members are of all ages.

Int'l Friendship League
22 Batterymarch St.
Boston, MA 02109

Int'l Pen Friends
P.O. Box 340
Dublin 12, Ireland

International Youth Service is one of the world's largest pen pal organizations especially for kids aged 10 to 20. The service is fast (you'll get a reply within two weeks) and costs 80¢ per name. You must order at least four names, so if the price is too steep get together with a few friends to send in the registration form. Write first for information to:

If you're 11 to 18 years old you can get a pen pal in a foreign country or within the United States or Canada through the Student Letter Exchange. A name in another country costs 65¢, a U.S. name costs 25¢, and you may choose the country or state in which you'd like a friend. Send a SASE for an order blank to:

Int'l Youth Service
P.B. 125
SF-20101 Turku 10
Finland

A letter from the U.S. to Canada or Mexico costs the same as a letter anywhere within the U.S.

A letter to any other country (outside North America) costs slightly more and should be weighed and stamped (with airmail stamps) at the post office.

Student Letter Exchange
R.F.D. #4
Waseca, MN 56093

World Pen Pal's slogan is "For Friendship, Understanding, and Peace." If you're 12 to 20 years old, $1 gets you one foreign name, a suggestion sheet, and a copy of *Write In There*, a pen pal newsletter.

World Pen Pals
1690 Como Ave.
St. Paul, MN 55108

I
I did
I did this
I did this to
I did this to take
I did this to take up
I did this to take up
                    space.

126

Writing Your Pen Pal

- Write your pen pal as soon as you receive his or her name and address.
- Lost names and addresses can't be replaced, so copy your pen pal's in the back of *SWAK* and in one other safe place.
- For overseas pen pals you may wish to use aerogrammes—stationery, envelope, and postage all-in-one—available at any post office.
- Write neatly and clearly. Remember, English may be a foreign language to your pen pal.
- Include your full name and address on both the letter and the envelope. Don't use abbreviations.
- When you get a letter from your new pen pal, write back quickly. A regular exchange of letters is important to both you and your friend.

WRITING TO FAMOUS PEOPLE

Who are your favorite rock stars? Why not write them letters and let them know?

Is a certain sports hero your personal choice for "Athlete of the Year?" Why not tell him or her yourself?

Would you like to tell the president of the United States what *you* think about what's going on in the world? Why not make your opinions known in a letter.

You can write to almost anyone. What's more, many of those famous people will write back!

Writing the Letter

First, think about whom you would like to write: musician or movie star, sports personality or politician, astronaut or artist, dancer or diplomat, author or royalty. Use your best stationery. Take your time and think about what you want to say. Be polite and complimentary; state your opinions and feelings. Talk about your interest in the person's activities and accomplishments. If you ask a thoughtful question you may be more likely to get a reply.

If you'd like a photo or an autograph, say so. Also, if you enclose a SASE you may get a response more quickly. (You needn't use a SASE when writing public officials.)

Famous people get many letters. You can make yours special by enclosing something extra—a drawing, cartoon, poem, or something else that you made yourself.

Find the Address

You can send letters to famous people in care of the places they work. Write to singers in care of their record companies, TV stars in care of their studios, athletes in care of their home stadiums, authors in care of their publishers, and so on.

These addresses are easy to get from the reference department of your public library.

GREETING:

Dear Mr. President,

The President
The White House
Washington, DC 20500

Public Officials

Let your public officials know what you think about education, kids' rights, conservation, the environment, energy policy, and national and international affairs. A congressperson or senator thinks of each letter he or she receives as representing about 500 opinions, so every letter is read carefully. Until you're 18 years old and can register to vote, letters to the president, your state governor, senators, congresspeople, and the editor of your local newspaper are your best way to influence the government process.

GREETING:

**Dear Governor
(last name),**

The Honorable
(Governor's name)
Governor of (State)
State Capitol Bldg.
(City, State, ZIP)

GREETING:

**Dear Senator
(last name),**

**The Honorable
(Senator's name)
United States Senate
Washington, DC 20510**

GREETING:

**Dear Mr. or Ms.
(Representative's
last name),**

**The Honorable
(Representative's name)
House of Representatives
Washington, DC 20515**

Write to the editor of your local newspaper when you want to share opinions with your fellow citizens. Newspapers publish clearly written, thoughtful letters. Page 2 or the editorial page of the newspaper usually contains its mailing address.

Astronauts

When astronauts have their feet on the ground they pick up their postcard mail care of:

**NASA
Johnson Space Center
Houston, TX 77058**

Cartoonists

Write to cartoonists in care of the newspaper or comic book in which you read their comics.

129

TV and Movie Stars

If you can't get to a *Who's Who* but know the studio where your favorite star works (you can find out by watching the closing credits of his or her movie or TV show) address your letter to that studio in care of the Public Relations Department. Be sure to include the name of the star and the program or film he or she appeared in on the envelope.

Television

ABC*
1330 Ave. of the Americas
New York, NY 10019

ABC Television Center
4151 Prospect Ave.
Los Angeles, CA 90027

CBS*
51 W. 52nd St.
New York, NY 10019

CBS Television City
7800 Beverly Blvd.
Los Angeles, CA 90036

Canadian Broadcasting
    Corp.
1500 Bronson Ave.
Ottawa, ON
K1G 3J5

Children's Television
    Workshop
One Lincoln Plaza
New York, NY 10023

MGM Television
10202 W. Washington
    Blvd.
Culver City, CA 90230

MTM Enterprises
4024 N. Radford Ave.
Studio City, CA 91604

Metromedia
485 Lexington Ave.
New York, NY 10017

NBC*
30 Rockefeller Plaza
New York, NY 10020

NBC-TV
3000 W. Alameda Ave.
Burbank, CA 91505

Public Broadcasting Service
    (PBS)
475 L'Enfant Plaza, N.W.
Washington, DC 20024

*For letters to soap opera and news personalities.

Paramount Television
5451 Marathon St.
Hollywood, CA 90038

TAT Communications
1901 Ave. of the Stars
Los Angeles, CA 90067

20th Century-Fox Television
Box 900
Beverly Hills, CA 90213

Universal Television
Universal Studios
Universal City, CA 91608

Walt Disney Productions
500 Buena Vista
Burbank, CA 91505

Westinghouse Broadcasting
    (Group W)
90 Park Ave.
New York, NY 10016

Movies

Avco Embassy Pictures Corp.
300 E. 42nd St.
New York, NY 10017

Columbia Pictures
1 Columbia Plaza
Burbank, CA 91505

20th Century-Fox Film Corp.
P.O. Box 900
Beverly Hills, CA 90213

United Artists Corp.
729 Seventh Ave.
New York, NY 10010

Universal Pictures
100 Universal City Plaza
Universal City, CA 91608

Warner Brothers
4000 Warner Blvd.
Burbank, CA 91505

Athletes

Write to individual athletes in care of their teams. Here are some addresses:

Baseball

Commissioner's
Office—Baseball
75 Rockefeller Plaza
New York, NY 10019

National League Office
1 Rockefeller Plaza
New York, NY 10020

Atlanta Braves
P.O. Box 4064
Atlanta, GA 30302

Chicago Cubs
Wrigley Field
Chicago, IL 60613

Cincinnati Reds
100 Riverfront Stadium
Cincinnati, OH 45202

Houston Astros
Astrodome
P.O. Box 288
Houston, TX 77001

Los Angeles Dodgers
Dodger Stadium
1000 Elysian Park Ave.
Los Angeles, CA 90012

Montreal Expos
P.O. Box 500, Station M
Montreal, Quebec
H1V 3P2

New York Mets
Shea Stadium
Roosevelt Ave. & 126th St.
Flushing, NY 11368

Philadelphia Phillies
P.O. Box 7575
Philadelphia, PA 19101

Pittsburgh Pirates
600 Stadium Circle
Pittsburgh, PA 15212

St. Louis Cardinals
Busch Memorial
    Stadium
250 Stadium Plaza
St. Louis, MO 63102

San Diego Padres
P.O. Box 2000
San Diego, CA 92120

San Francisco Giants
Candlestick Park
San Francisco, CA 94124

American League Office
280 Park Ave.
New York, NY 10017

Baltimore Orioles
Memorial Stadium
Baltimore, MD 21218

Boston Red Sox
24 Yawkey Way
Boston, MA 02215

California Angels
Anaheim Stadium
2000 State College Blvd.
Anaheim, CA 92806

Chicago White Sox
Comisky Park
Dan Ryan & 35th St.
Chicago, IL 60616

Cleveland Indians
Cleveland Stadium
Cleveland, OH 44114

Detroit Tigers
Tiger Stadium
Detroit, MI 48216

Kansas City Royals
Harry S. Truman Sports
    Complex
P.O. Box 1969
Kansas City, MO 64141

Milwaukee Brewers
Milwaukee County
    Stadium
Milwaukee, WI 53214

Minnesota Twins
Metropolitan Stadium
8001 Cedar Ave.
Bloomington, MN 55420

New York Yankees
Yankee Stadium
Bronx, NY 10451

Oakland A's
Oakland-Alameda
    County Coliseum
Oakland, CA 94621

Seattle Mariners
P.O. Box 4100
Seattle, WA 98104

Texas Rangers
Arlington Stadium
P.O. Box 1111
Arlington, TX 76010

Toronto Blue Jays
Box 7777
Adelaide St. P.O.
Toronto, ON
M5C 2K7

Basketball

NBA Office
Olympic Tower
645 Fifth Ave.
New York, NY 10022

Atlanta Hawks
100 Techwood Dr., N.W.
Atlanta, GA 30303

Boston Celtics
Boston Garden
North Station
Boston, MA 02114

Chicago Bulls
333 N. Michigan Ave.
Chicago, IL 60601

Cleveland Cavaliers
The Coliseum
2923 Streetsboro Rd.
Richfield, OH 44286

Dallas Mavericks
6830 Dartbrook
Dallas, TX 75240

Denver Nuggets
P.O. Box 4286
Denver, CO 80204

Detroit Pistons
Pontiac Silverdome
1200 Featherstone
Pontiac, MI 48057

Golden State Warriors
Oakland Coliseum Arena
Oakland, CA 94621

Houston Rockets
The Summit
Houston, TX 77046

Indiana Pacers
Market Square Center
151 N. Delaware
Indianapolis, IN 46204

Kansas City Kings
1800 Genessee
Kansas City, MO 64102

Los Angeles Lakers
The Forum
3900 W. Manchester Blvd.
or P.O. Box 10
Inglewood, CA 90306

Milwaukee Bucks
901 N. 4th St.
Milwaukee, WI 53203

New Jersey Nets
185 E. Union Ave.
E. Rutherford, NJ 07073

New York Knicks
Madison Square Garden
4 Pennsylvania Plaza
New York, NY 10001

Philadelphia 76ers
Veterans Stadium
P.O. Box 25040
Philadelphia, PA 19147

Phoenix Suns
P.O. Box 1369
Phoenix, AZ 85001

Portland Trail Blazers
Lloyd Bldg.
700 N.E. Multnomah St.
Portland, OR 97232

San Antonio Spurs
Hernis Fair Arena
P.O. Box 530
San Antonio, TX 78292

San Diego Clippers
San Diego Sports Arena
3500 Sports Arena Blvd.
San Diego, CA 92110

Seattle SuperSonics
419 Occidental S.
Seattle, WA 98104

Utah Jazz
Salt Palace
100 S.W. Temple
Salt Lake City, UT 84101

Washington Bullets
1 Harry S. Truman Dr.
Landover, MD 20786

Hockey

NHL Headquarters
960 Sun Life Bldg.
Montreal, Quebec
H3B 2W2

Boston Bruins
150 Causeway St.
Boston, MA 02114

Buffalo Sabres
Memorial Auditorium
Buffalo, NY 14202

Calgary Flames
1500 Home Oil Tower
Calgary, Alta.
T2P 2Z2

Chicago Black Hawks
1800 W. Madison St.
Chicago, IL 60612

Colorado Rockies
McNichols Sports Arena
Denver, CO 80204

Detroit Red Wings
5920 Grand River Ave.
Detroit, MI 48208

Edmonton Oilers
Edmonton Coliseum
Edmonton, Alta.
T5B 4M9

Hartford Whalers
One Civic Center Plaza
Hartford, CT 06103

Los Angeles Kings
P.O. Box 10
Inglewood, CA 90306

Minnesota North Stars
7901 Cedar Ave. S.
Bloomington, MN 55420

Montreal Canadiens
2313 St. Catherine St. W.
Montreal, QB
H3H 1N2

New York Islanders
Nassau Coliseum
Uniondale, NY 11553

New York Rangers
Madison Square Garden
4 Pennsylvania Plaza
New York, NY 10001

Philadelphia Flyers
The Spectrum
Pattison Place
Philadelphia, PA 19148

Pittsburgh Penguins
Civic Arena
Pittsburgh, PA 15219

Quebec Nordiques
5555 Bierne Ave. Ouest
Charlesbourg, QB
G1H 6R1

St. Louis Blues
5700 Oakland Ave.
St. Louis, MO 63110

Toronto Maple Leafs
60 Carlton St.
Toronto, ON
M5B 1L1

Vancouver Canucks
100 N. Renfrew St.
Vancouver, BC
V5K 3N7

Washington Capitals
Capital Centre
Landover, MD 20786

Winnipeg Jets
15-1430 Maroons Rd.
Winnipeg, MB
R3G 0L5

Football

NFL Office
410 Park Ave.
New York, NY 10022

Atlanta Falcons
Suwanee Rd.
Suwanee, GA 30174

Baltimore Colts
Executive Plaza
Hunt Valley, MD 21031

Buffalo Bills
1 Bills Drive
Orchard Park, NY 14127

Chicago Bears
55 E. Jackson Blvd.
Chicago, IL 60604

Cincinnati Bengals
200 Riverfront Stadium
Cincinnati, OH 45202

Cleveland Browns
Cleveland Stadium
Cleveland, OH 44114

Dallas Cowboys
6116 N. Central Expwy.
Dallas, TX 75206

Denver Broncos
5700 Logan St.
Denver, CO 80216

Detroit Lions
1200 Featherstone Rd.
Box 4200
Pontiac, MI 48507

Green Bay Packers
1285 Lombardi Ave.
Green Bay, WI 54303

Houston Oilers
P.O. Box 1516
Houston, TX 77001

Kansas City Chiefs
1 Arrowhead Dr.
Kansas City, MO 64129

Los Angeles Rams
10271 W. Pico Blvd.
Los Angeles, CA 90064

Miami Dolphins
330 Biscayne Blvd.
Miami, FL 33132

Minnesota Vikings
7110 France Ave. S.
Edna, MN 55435

New England Patriots
Schaefer Stadium
Foxboro, MA 02035

New Orleans Saints
1500 Poydras St.
New Orleans, LA 70112

New York Giants
Giants Stadium
E. Rutherford, NJ 07073

New York Jets
598 Madison Ave.
New York, NY 10022

Oakland Raiders
7811 Oakport St.
Oakland, CA 94621

Philadelphia Eagles
Veterans Stadium
Philadelphia, PA 19148

Pittsburgh Steelers
Three Rivers Stadium
Pittsburgh, PA 15212

St. Louis Cardinals
200 Stadium Plaza
St. Louis, MO 63102

San Diego Chargers
San Diego Stadium
P.O. Box 20666
San Diego, CA 92120

San Francisco 49ers
711 Nevada St.
Redwood City, CA 94061

Seattle Seahawks
5305 Lake Washington Blvd.
Kirkland, WA 96033

Tampa Bay Buccaneers
1 Buccaneer Place
Tampa, FL 83607

Washington Redskins
P.O. Box 17247
Dulles Intl. Airport
Washington, DC 20041

Soccer

League Office
1133 Ave. of the Americas
Suite 3500
New York, NY 10036

Atlanta Chiefs
P.O. Box 5015
Atlanta, GA 30302

California Surf
P.O. Box 4449
Anaheim, CA 92603

Chicago Sting
Suite 1525
333 N. Michigan Ave.
Chicago, IL 60601

Dallas Tornado
6116 N. Central Expwy.
Dallas, TX 75206

Detroit Express
Pontiac Silverdome
1200 Featherstone Rd.
Pontiac, MI 48057

Edmonton Drillers
10039 Jasper Ave.
Edmonton, Alta.
T5J 1T4

Ft. Lauderdale Strikers
1350 N.E. 56th St.
Ft. Lauderdale, FL 33334

Houston Hurricanes
P.O. Box 27229
Houston, TX 77042

Low Angeles Aztecs
777 Rose Bowl Dr.
Pasadena, CA 91103

Memphis Rogues
2200 Union Ave.
Memphis, TN 36104

Minnesota Kicks
7200 France Ave. S.
Minneapolis, MN 55435

New England Tea Men
34 Mechanic St.
Foxboro, MA 02035

New York Cosmos
75 Rockefeller Plaza
New York, NY 10019

Philadelphia Fury
Veterans Stadium
Broad St. & Pattison Ave.
Philadelphia, PA 19148

Portland Timbers
910 S.W. 18th
Portland, OR 97205

Rochester Lancers
812 Wilder Bldg.
Rochester, NY 14614

San Diego Sockers
San Diego Stadium
9449 Friars Rd.
San Diego, CA 92108

San Jose Earthquakes
Suite 272
2025 Gateway Place
San Jose, CA 95110

Seattle Sounders
419 Occidental S.
Seattle, WA 98104

Tampa Bay Rowdies
Suite 109
1311 N. West Shore Blvd.
Tampa, FL 33607

Toronto Blizzard
Exhibition Stadium
Toronto, ON
M8K 3C3

Tulsa Roughnecks
P.O. Box 35190
Tulsa, OK 75135

Vancouver Whitecaps
3683 E. Hastings St.
Vancouver, BC
V5K 2B1

Washington Diplomats
RFK Stadium
E. Capitol St. & 22nd NE
Washington, DC 20003

Tips from a Veteran Autograph Hound

Fourteen-year-old Tom Kielty has been collecting autographs for several years now, mostly by mail. With more than 200 autographs in his collection, Tom, a sports fan, prizes most the letters and signed photographs sent by favorite athletes. Here are some of Tom's tips for writing for autographs:

■ A friendly letter written on lined paper is fine.

■ When writing to sports figures, write to your favorite player on a team (not to the whole team). Tell the person that he or she is your favorite and why. Tell about yourself. If you're involved in the same sport, say so. Write about your team—its name, your position, how often you play, and other stuff.

■ When writing to politicians and public officials state your opinions on various issues.

■ If you want an autographed photo, ask for it.

■ Try to write to sportspeople off season. Players usually have more time to answer mail then.

■ Be patient. You usually have to wait four to six weeks for a reply.

■ Always write down useful addresses when you see them in newspapers, magazines, and other places. (Write them down in the back of *SWAK*.)

134

DISCOVER MAIL ART

If you like to draw, paint, write poetry, make collages and other art, here is a way you can share your work with other artists and see what they're doing too. Mail art (also called correspondence art or postal art) is a huge pen pal system of artists of all ages and nationalities, most of whom have never met, who exchange their work and ideas through the mail. It's fun and adventurous because once you begin sending your artwork to others, you never know what surprise will turn up in your mailbox next.

Read on to find out about a few artists with whom you could begin a correspondence. Each one may send you names and addresses of other artists who have something in common with you. That's how you get in to the "eternal network," as mail art is called.

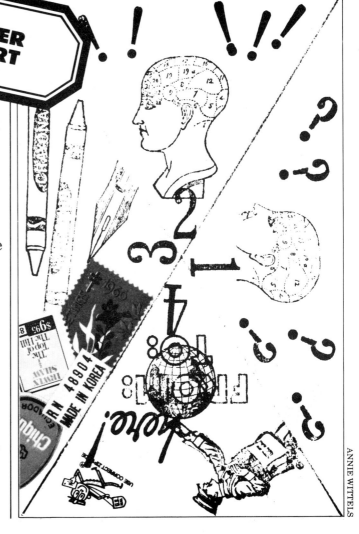

ANNIE WITTELS

The World's Youngest Mail Artist

Lee Spiegelman, born on September 23, 1977, may be the world's youngest mail artist. He makes art with his father, Lon Spiegelman, who corresponds with over 500 artists and has had his work shown in more than 200 postal art exhibitions. Lon says, "Mail artists, for the most part, do not make money from their mail-work . . . they give it away. They share it. They trade it. This is part of the joy of mail art. It's like Christmas every day." Exchange some of your art with the Spiegelmans.

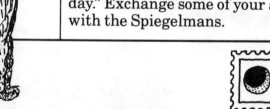

Lon and Lee Spiegelman
1556 Elevado St.
Los Angeles, CA 90026

The Cracker Jack Kid

Chuck Welch has put together national exhibitions of postal art by junior and senior high school students. If you are interested, contact him for current information on exhibitions in schools.

Chuck, who goes by the "mail handle" Cracker Jack Kid, believes that mail art is for everybody. To anyone who sends him art he promises to return "a surprise in every mailbox."

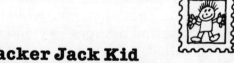

Cracker Jack Kid
2468 S. Third St. Plz.
Omaha, NE 68108

Go Bananas!

Anna Banana is one of mail art's best-loved personalities. Her banana postcards and rubber stamps are only a small part of the imaginative projects she creates. In 1980 she even staged an International Banana Olympics.

One of Anna's current projects is putting together her *Encyclopedia Bananica*, a big book of everything you ever wanted to know about bananas. You guessed it, she's collecting information through the mail.

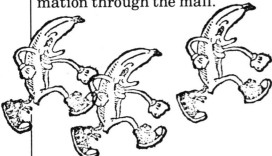

If you have any banana stories, pictures, personal anecdotes, jokes, cartoons, poems, or anything else (make something up)

for the *Bananica*, send it with a SASE to:

**Anna Banana
P.O. Box 11739
San Francisco, CA 94101**

She will send you a Master's Degree of Bananology in return for your contribution. (Anna travels a lot and can't always answer right away, so don't worry if you don't get your degree immediately. It'll come.)

Mail Art Shows

Many mail art exhibitions (shows) are put on each year. The organizers (usually artists) first select a theme for the show — something simple like "flamingos" or more complex like "alien transmissions."

After setting a deadline several months away, they publicize their show in art magazines (such as *Umbrella*, P.O. Box 3692, Glendale, CA 91201) and invite all the artists they know to send work. When the deadline arrives (along with lots of mail art) the show is put on display in a gallery or other public space for a certain amount of time. Sometimes artwork submitted is printed in catalogs and sent to artists who contributed work.

Anyone can enter mail art shows. All work is displayed, but usually no work is returned. (The organizers of the show keep the art together as a whole.) Contributors get the satisfaction of having their work displayed and viewed in faraway places, plus seeing what other artists made when the catalog arrives.

If you would like a list of current mail art show deadlines or other kids with whom to exchange artwork, write to:

SASE

**Mail Art
P.O. Box 152
Barrington, RI 02806**

Enclose a SASE, and a note to say what interests you.

JAMES FELTER

STUDIO LeCLAIR

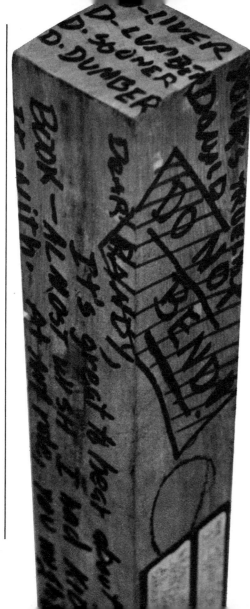

A Post via Post

The author of this book received lots of mail art while *SWAK* was being written, but none amazed the post office (or the author) more than a 2-foot long, 4-by-4-inch board sent by New York artist Donald Lipski. This post (get it?) arrived with the address label and stamps stuck right on the wood and the following message written on the board with a marker: "Tell them that I said it's OK to send things through the mail other than cards and letters! I once sent a blown-out eggshell, but it never got there . . . A friend once sent a balloon—she just wrote the address right on the balloon with Magic Marker and glued the stamp on with Elmer's glue. I bet it raised a few eyebrows down at the post office. Yours truly, Donald."

The sturdy 6-pound board was marked "Fragile," "Do Not Bend," and "D-liver/ D-lumber/ D-sooner/ D-dumber."

Many children's magazines, such as *Cricket*, *Dynamite*, and *Boys' Life*, devote several pages to original work by kids. Some print drawings, stories, puzzles, riddles and jokes they receive. Some sponsor literary and art contests. Almost all print interesting letters from their readers. With a variety of good kids' publications around today, there are many opportunities for young authors and artists to get their work published. Read your favorite magazines carefully for their instructions about sending original material.

Many publishers have a policy of "no returns." If you submit something, do not send away your only copy. If you type, keep a carbon copy. If you don't type, print your manuscript neatly and make a photocopy.

A Monthly Called Boing!

Boing! is a national newspaper by, for, and about kids. Its national headquarters is the Children's Museum of Denver (Colorado), but many kids' museums across America add articles and artwork gathered from children in their area. (The paper is distributed by the local museums.) For more information write to:

Boing!
The Children's Museum
of Denver
931 Bannock St.
Denver, CO 80204

SASE

An Editor's Tips

Janice O'Donnell, editor for the Rhode Island edition of *Boing!*, loves getting kids' work for the newspaper. "We editors like getting letters and stuff from kids. It lets us know they're reading and enjoying our publication. Please, keep writing!"

She offers these tips for artists and writers who want to get published:

- First, always remember to include your full name and address with anything you send.
- Of the artwork submitted, editors are most likely to use single-color drawings because they reproduce best in black and white.
- When you write, be honest. Say what you really think and feel, not what you think others want to hear.
- Be patient. Months may pass from the time you send your work till you hear whether it will be published. (It takes a long time to put together something for publication.)
- Editors are very busy people. Although they'd like to, they seldom find time to call or write contributors. If you want your work returned, enclose a SASE.

Q. What kind of letters did Rapunzel like best?
A. Hair mail.

Q. What does an envelope say when you lick it?
A. Not one word. It just shuts up.

A Magazine by Kids

Stone Soup is an excellent magazine of stories, poems, book reviews, and pictures by children aged 6 to 12 from all over the United States and Canada. The editors encourage kids to take their literary and artistic skills seriously and to approach their subjects with honesty, sensitivity, and care.

Submit your original work for possible publication. Be sure your name and age is on each piece, and if you want your work returned enclose a SASE. Send submissions to:

Stone Soup
P.O. Box 83
Santa Cruz, CA 95063

Your Art on Greeting Cards

Hello Studio™ specializes in publishing children's art on their greeting cards, called the Children's Art Collection®. The artists that run Hello Studio believe that all children can create, and that kids should be recognized as writers and artists.

> *"We invite all young artists, poets, authors, joke and riddle makers to send in their original work for possible publication. Include name, age, and address. Sorry no material can be returned, all material submitted become the exclusive property of Hello Studio, Inc. Thank you."*

The invitation above is printed on the back of every greeting card. Not every kid's work can be published, but *every* child who submits original work receives a certificate "to show everybody that you are one of the great masters of tomorrow."

If Hello Studio does publish your work, your name will be printed on all the cards and you and your parents will get a box of cards to keep and use.

Also, donations to help needy children are made from the proceeds of every card.

Over 600 kids have already had their work published by Hello Studio, and thousands of others have certificates to prove their work has been received and appreciated by professional artists who know that kids *are* the great masters of tomorrow.

Send your work to:

The Children's Art Collection
Hello Studio, Inc.
Fleischmanns, NY 12430

ON THE ROAD

Before you and your family take off on vacation, you can get pictures, maps, and information about where you're going to help you plan your trip. Send your request to the chamber of commerce of the city or the tourist information office of the country, state, or province that is your destination.

For a list of specific addresses for U.S. state tourist offices send your request and a SASE to:

Travel Development Division Travel Industry Assoc. of America 1899 L St., NW Washington, DC 20036

For information about Canadian vacations write to:

Canada Government Office of Tourism 150 Kent St. Ottawa, ON K1A 0H6

For a list of addresses for information offices of various countries send your request to:

Office of Public Information United Nations New York, NY 10017

SASE

Souvenirs!

Wherever you go, send your friends souvenirs of your trip: drawings and snapshots of special places and events, souvenir menus and paper placemats, tourist folders, and, of course, postcards. Postmarks are mementos too, so if you pass through Flamingo, Florida, or any other town with a great name, be sure to mail some postcards from the local post office. (If you place it in a mailbox instead, you may not get the local postmark that you want.)

When you visit a foreign country send home picture postcards with beautiful stamps to *yourself*! Jot a few lines about what you're up to that day (write to "Dear Diary" if you like). When you get home a fine souvenir will be waiting in your mailbox: a picture, foreign stamp, postmark with date — a special written memory all in one!

SUMMER CAMP

Mail Call!

What would summer camp be without mail call?!? Make sure you get lots of mail at camp by letting all your friends and relatives know, before you leave, your camp address and the exact dates you'll be there. Ask your best friends to send letters three days *before you leave* so you'll have mail the first day—your bunkmates will be amazed!

Just as during the rest of the year, the more mail you send, the more mail you'll get. Use the arts and crafts shop to create crazy, memorable mail such as the popsicle-stick postcard on this page.

While you're learning about nature in the wilds of Camp Whatchamacallit, share your discoveries with your family and friends back home by enclosing natural surprises in your letters: pressed leaves and flowers, feathers, and so forth. *Do not* send examples of poison ivy or samples of camp food (yuk!).

All the ideas in *SWAK* will make camp mail more fun, so *pack this book!*

Round Robins!

Mail is the best way to continue the fun of camp when the summer is over. Start a round robin with the other kids in your cabin or your closest group of friends. (Any group of three or more people can do a round robin, of course; not only campers.) Here's how:

While you're still at camp, exchange addresses and decide on a round robin route. For example:

Ann

Beth   Deb

Cathy

When everybody gets home, Ann writes the first letter to "Dear Everybody." She mails it to Beth.

When Beth gets it, she writes a letter to everybody and puts both Ann's and her letter in one envelope and mails them to Cathy.

Cathy adds her own letter and sends all three to Deb.

Deb adds her letter and sends all four to Ann.

Now Ann gets four letters in one envelope, and one of them is hers. She removes her letter, writes a new one, and sends all four on to Beth.

Each time a person gets the round robin she (or he) takes out her last correspondence and adds something new. Usually friends make a rule that each person can only keep the round robin for a certain amount of time (say three days) before mailing it on. It's called a round robin because it goes round and round for as long as everybody likes.

Include snapshots and other stuff to make your letter more fun — you'll get it back when the round robin returns.

Start a drawing or story and send it along with your letter with a request that your friends add to it. You're in for a surprise when it gets back to you!

147

ZIP

Name

Address

ZIP

Name

Address

ZIP

Name

Address

ZIP

Name

Address

ZIP

Name

Address

ZIP

Name

Address

ZIP

Name

Address

ZIP

149

Name

Address

ZIP

Name

Address

ZIP

Name

Address

ZIP

Name

Address

150 ZIP

Name

Address

ZIP

Name

Address

ZIP

Name

Address

ZIP

Name

Address

ZIP

Q. What word has hundreds of letters in it?

A. Mailbox.

151

Name

Address

ZIP

Name

Address

ZIP

Name

Address

ZIP

Name

Address

ZIP